HIGHLIGHTS OF A LOWLIFE

HIGHLIGHTS OF A LOWLIFE

The Autobiography of Milan Melvin

Compiled and edited by Peter Laufer

JORVIK P R E S S

ISBN-10: 0986377007
ISBN-13: 978-0-9863770-0-6

A private edition of this book was published
by Swan Isle Books in 2004 under
the Library of Congress
Catalog No: 2004090820

Cover photo of Milan Melvin
in San Francisco, 1969,
by Baron Wolman

Cover design: Keith Carlson

Second edition

Jorvik Press
PMB 424, 5331 SW Macadam Ave., Ste. 258,
Portland OR 97239
JorvikPress.com

ABOUT THE EDITOR

An independent journalist, broadcaster and documentary filmmaker, Peter Laufer is the James Wallace Chair in Journalism at the University of Oregon School of Journalism and Communication.

He took his first radio job while in high school at one of the early all-talk radio stations, KNEW in Oakland. From there he moved to KSFO San Francisco as a news writer and in 1970 took a cable car to the studios of KSAN, the famous (and infamous) Jive 95, co-founded by the subject of this book, where he joined the news department as a reporter.

As news reporter, talk show host, bureau chief, and news and program director, Laufer has since worked for radio stations and media networks throughout the US and Europe. He reported, wrote and produced documentaries and special event broadcasts as a globe-trotting correspondent for NBC News and also covered major European news stories for CBS Radio.

His print journalism has appeared in *SF Weekly, San Francisco Examiner, New York Times, Washington Post, Europe* magazine, *Mother Jones, Hungry Mind Review, Washington Journalism Review, Kansas City Star, Fort Worth Star-Telegram, San Francisco Chronicle,* and *Pozor* magazine (Prague). His work as reporter, writer and producer of documentary films includes *Exodus to Berlin* (with Jeff Kamen), *Sea to Shining Sea,* a portrait of immediate post-9/11 Middle America, and *Garbage,* a biography of household trash.

After studying at UC Berkeley, he earned his Master's in Communications: Journalism and Public Affairs from the American University in Washington DC and his PhD in Cultural Studies from Leeds Metropolitan University in England, followed by post-graduate studies in Germany, France and Spain.

A frequent speaker and guest lecturer on media subjects around the world, Peter Laufer has written, co-authored or edited over 20 books.

ACKNOWLEDGMENTS

Many people contributed to this posthumous autobiography of Milan Melvin with their memories shared through letters, emails, phone calls and photographs.

The editor and publishers would like to thank all who made this book possible, especially Janelle Melvin, Carl Gottlieb, Larry Hankin, Hugh Romney (aka Wavy Gravy), David Crosby, Howard Hesseman, Alan Myerson, Mike Wilhelm and Ben Fong-Torres.

Special thanks to Baron Wolman, Carrie Kania of Iconic Images, and Lisa Law for their generous help with photographs.

All I really want to do is roam the world and one day write the great autobiographical book.

Milan Melvin in a 1970 letter home
to his sister Janelle, postmarked Paris

Remember, between the mind and the hand lies the elbow.

Milan Melvin in a 1975 letter home
offering sage advice to his friend Peter Laufer

CONTENTS

FOREWORD TO THE SECOND EDITION

Suffocating in the 37 degrees here in my Vienna flat as I draft this foreword to the second edition of my old friend's autobiography. What is that in American Fahrenheit? Well into the triple digits, perhaps. That's certainly how it feels. But with no conversion chart or Google cheat sheet handy, I'll just call it what it is: *Scheiße heiß*.

I often think of Milan when I'm working in Europe. He and I first encountered one another in Paris – though we both were ingredients of the strange brew laboring at the microphones of San Francisco's ultimate underground radio station, KSAN. We met on a peniché moored at the Quai de Conti between Pont Neuf and Pont des Arts in the shadow of Notre Dame.

I'm convinced Milan would embrace those descriptions: in the shadow of Notre Dame and ultimate underground radio. He appreciated framing the moment. He called his life his art. And he talked about those moments he discovered and created as his art that built his legends.

I wear a treasure from one of those legends every day, the stone – gold-flaked lapis lazuli – that he smuggled out of Afghanistan for my (and one for Sheila's) wedding ring. That was long before most Americans could find Kabul on a world map, back when Afghanistan was a code word in journalism for stories too obscure to merit coverage in a hometown newspaper when the local news gets short shrift.

Milan thrived on breaking new ground while lighting for Huck Finn's territory.

I'm writing these memories with a pen in a notebook – longhand, just as Milan and I corresponded back in those pre-email days, scribbling our ideas and reflections on the pale-blue aerograms that lazily floated by post between our oft-disparate ports of call (pre-Skype international phone calls were stunningly expensive and saved for crises).

Dismissive words from Milan in one of those exchanges come to mind whenever I'm intrigued here in Europe by some cultural oddity that differs from our own American variation. "Everything west of Istanbul," he sniffed, "is just a suburb of LA."

Arguably so. One of the values of Milan's autobiography, besides the insight it offers into a unique American character sallying about his world, is its historical snapshot of a time when American-style global consumer culture had not yet infested most everywhere. At last report there was no McDonald's in Kathmandu, but Milan likely would be horrified and/or amused to see the Kentucky Fried Chicken outlet in the Blue Bird Mall (free delivery to Milan's old Kathmandu quarters, promises the Colonel – even though he's been excommunicated by his corporate descendants).

Hence, as custodian of and editor for Milan's autobiographical notes, news dispatches, tales and memorabilia, I was most pleased when Peter Stansill and Hammond Guthrie contacted me from their Portland-based publishing house. Their desire to add Milan Melvin's trips through our times to the Jorvik Press list means that a high-quality edition of Milan's autobiography long will be available to both Sixties survivors and new generations of readers.

And wherever he currently is adventuring, when my pal Milan receives that news, he will smile, knowing that his legacy of legends continues...

Peter Laufer
Josefstadt, Wien, 2015

INTRODUCTION

The late days of summer, 2001. Around the world, life goes on. Suddenly and unexpectedly from Oakland to Kathmandu, from Bali to Hollywood, from Paris to Puerto Vallarta, Mexico, the magic of the Internet instantaneously cries out with this email from Milan Morrell Melvin to his huge cast of friends and family worldwide:

8 August 2001

Well, the results of my CT scan-guided-biopsy are in and I learned of them in the most bizarre way.

I was relaxing on pins and needles in my hospital room, awaiting the report with my sister, Janelle. I was also expecting a schedule for the surgery to remove what we all expected to be a problematic spleen. I sent a request to the doctor for a pass to leave the hospital to attend Mimi Farina's memorial at Grace but the nurse brought the reply that I wouldn't need a pass because the doctor would be releasing me and was on his way to talk to me!

Dr. Lawrence Way, honcho professor of surgery at UCSF, explained that the pathology report showed that I have cancer of the pancreas and that it has metastasized to such as extent that it makes no sense to operate and remove any one organ in particular because it was all over inside. In response to the obvious "How long do I have?" question, he responded, "With treatment, a year."

So I sped over to Grace Cathedral and found myself in the strange position of saying to friends, "Yes, it's tragic about Mimi but I'm so relieved she's out of pain after such a torturous final two years and... uh... and minutes ago I was diagnosed with pancreatic cancer."

That was a mouthful to which my pal Eric Christensen responded, "How ironic."

The good news is that there was such a concentration of close friends to commiserate with me that it cushioned the shock and, frankly, filled my commiseration quota to overflowing.

Philosophical gut check was next. No, I'm not afraid to die. I've flirted with her all my adult life and she doesn't scare me. Matter of fact, I almost embrace the idea. The next adventure and ultimate mystery, no? Besides, I look forward to my conversations with Albert Einstein, Mohandas Gandhi, Emiliano Zapata and Mimi Farina.

Here on the earthly plane, I will leave behind me a very strong business (in partnership with Georgeanne in Bali and Yoli in Mexico) that, if handled as I've handled it in this past, will provide a great income for scores of people for years to come.

Treatment-wise I'm still in the investigative stage, trying to determine if it's worth it or not to pursue which of the many options. I will not spend my last year on the planet chasing cures, waiting for more doctors to return calls and spending what could be a wonderful year of Freely Frolicking With Friends into a year of Desperately Dogging Doctors.

I'll keep you posted as news comes in; meanwhile, please know that we'll see one another again before this thing is over – I promise!

Love to you,

Milan

Milan and I were friends for over thirty years. I was on the list of those who received that sobering and sad message. As was the case with so many of us, for me Milan dying was difficult to believe. Not only was he relatively young, but he had led a death-defying life of mad adventure since before I met him. Perhaps he wasn't going to outlive us all, but it was beyond his living legend to consider he was about to succumb to something as mundane as sickness.

Had I heard he had been shot by smugglers and bandits, pushed out of a CIA helicopter by his superior officer, was rotting in a Third World prison charged with fomenting revolution, or had simply disappeared, it would have been much easier to accommodate than this pancreatic cancer diagnosis.

Milan was a Zelig-like figure for the latter half of the twentieth century. He seemed to be everywhere and do everything – and be there and do it first. From the postwar tedium of the paranoid Fifties, through the sex, drugs and rock-and-roll Sixties, on to the world-trekking Seventies, the self-reflective Eighties, the capital-building Nineties, Milan was a player, a teacher and always a student on the world stage.

In many ways, as his autobiography makes clear, he lived the Baby Boomer fantasy life: rarely compromising, highly political, self-indulgent, seeking enlightenment and instant gratification simultaneously.

A few weeks after that death-sentence email, I was stuck in Washington DC with all flights home to California grounded. It was September 2001, and I was wandering around looking at Humvees and National Guardsmen on patrol in Georgetown, watching the Pentagon smolder from the Key Bridge, when my mobile phone rang with a call from Milan in Mexico. He was dying faster than he had expected. In the midst of the national tragedy he and his friends and family were suffering a personal tragedy.

He told me he wanted me to come to Puerto Vallarta and debrief him. His memoirs were unfinished. He wanted these interviews to complete the story and then he wanted me to compile and edit the material.

"I don't want this job," I complained, still stunned at his diagnosis. For me, Milan was always like an invulnerable older brother.

He reminded me that when he first became sick I offered to do whatever he needed.

"Here's a lesson," he advised. "Be careful what you offer."

Over the next few weeks I made two trips to see him in Mexico. He talked as long as his strength lasted. Once in a while we laughed. He took me up to his dream ranch, where the workers were putting the finishing touches on his new house.

He told stories, ancient and contemporary.

Pointing to the laborers, he remembered when they were taking a break while finishing the roof. "Come on you assholes," the foreman had yelled at them. "We're not up north!" Milan clearly loved Mexico.

At his apartment in Puerto Vallarta he gave me a Zip drive filled with his stories, letters, emails and other notes for his autobiographical works. He asked me to retrieve boxes of more letters, photographs and other ephemeral material from his sister's basement in California.

We agreed I would compile the collection into the memoir he had always planned to write, adding commentary only when necessary to provide context, editing only for clarity.

Milan started to finish the project himself with these initial lines addressed directly to his son, Mocean:

Truth be told, Son, I don't know how much time I've got left on this keyboard of life here. Some days it feels like I've got years to go, other days I'm sure I can count the minutes till it crashes. I've got lots to tell you so I'm going fly through it and you can edit or rewrite it for your own kids, or not.

1

DEATH: THE ULTIMATE ADVENTURE

Milan was filled with stories during our last meetings in Puerto Vallarta. But first he agreed to talk about what was coming next. "It occurs to me," I suggested, "that perhaps you want to provide Mocean and others who read this with a window on your experiences of dying that could be of some value."

I don't know that I have any insights. I mean death happens to everybody and there's been a lot of more articulate people than I who've had a lot better things to say about death than I have. But my first reaction when I heard in the hospital that I had less than a year to live was a philosophical gut-check. Like, right off the bat, did that scare me? Was I afraid? And no, as a result of living with Tibetan people and absorbing their culture for five years, it doesn't scare me, I'm ready for that next level. I'm ready to go through the bardos. I'm ready to pop out the other side and start all over again because that, as I understand it, is just the nature of things.

So the first philosophical gut-check was fear. No, I'm not afraid of dying. The second emotion that crept up on me, and I was surprised, was anger. I was deeply angered by this development. All those questions that one naturally asks, like: Who signed the death warrant? Or: Why am I singled out when things are so good at a time when things are running so well, so good in my life. Why am I singled out to be removed from it? Where is the fairness when people like Dick Cheney can pop out of the hospital and go back to work? Why am I, who has been working towards building a virtual economic commune here where hundreds of people are benefiting from the work that we've done here, taken out of the picture?

But then I realized after a while there's nothing or no one to be angry at. If it were a matter of, say, I drank too many beers in my life and this beer had a poisonous preservative in it that made it last longer in the refrigerator, have a longer shelf life, and I could go after the beer company, then I would feel a focus for the anger. But this pancreatic cancer at this point, nobody has the first idea about where it comes from or why it starts or why it does what it does. So there's really nobody to be angry at. One has to give up that anger after a while, because there's no reason for it, no focus. Who's to be angry at? What's to be angry at? It doesn't do any good.

So then acceptance, acceptance is a point at which you focus on the things that you wanted to do in life before you check out. My most immediate goal was to ensure that this business that we've built here together will continue on because it makes so much money for so many people. My first priority was to organize things so that it would continue. My second priority was this book. My son has always asked me to tell him my stories and I've always let him down. I've always felt guilty for not telling him more stories.

He said to me, I can remember, at each, at every foot that he grew, "Dad, tell me a story about that. Tell me..."

"Well, I don't have time, son, you know?" I told him.

I've always let him down on the story-telling front. Now I want to pass these stories on to him. After that it's a matter of just how long can I manage the pain before I go. The pain is unbearable at times. The more morphine you take to try and assuage that pain, the more other things go wrong in your body and don't work, and you can't go to the bathroom and then you can't eat and then you get more pain and it's just a vicious, vicious circle. As soon as we finish the book it's a matter of just how long can I handle how much pain before I choose to go room temperature.

"Paws up, as you've also been saying," I tried to lighten the moment.

Before I go paws up, right.

"Who gets credit for paws up?" I asked.

It's on a list that Carl Gottlieb sent me.

"Before we leave this," I asked him, "what is in your heart and your mind and your soul as best you can tap that, regarding what's happening next? Where are you going?"

Oh, well, I don't know. And I'm intrigued by the mystery. Part of me wants to run to what I learned from the Tibetans, to the journey through the bardos to another incarnation. I know I've got a lot to learn. I know I've learned a lot and I'm not a bad guy, so I'm not going to get a bad incarnation. But I know I still have a lot more to learn as far as patience and compassion and anger management go. I guess I'll come back around and do it again. Part of me wants to run to that: the Tibetan passage through the bardos and next incarnation. I wish I'd spent more time with the Tibetans preparing for that trip through the bardos.

Part of it also is just the adventure of it. I mean who knows what's going on next? But I've done almost every kind of adventure that I know how to do on the planet. Maybe it's time for me to go on to this adventure.

Maybe that's why it's happening: because I need the next adventure, I don't know.

"You figure there is something else out there?"

Yeah, and if not there's nothing to lose, right? I mean one might as well look forward to it. I've always looked forward to the challenges and come through most of them pretty well.

"Does it give you a sense of comfort that you will be in a position to control the specificity of the exit time?"

Yes, absolutely. I always can do that. I can just go over the balcony there anytime I want. But with the help of a doctor down here I think I'm going be able to call the time at which I can just climb into bed and ask him to turn out the lights for me. There's a great deal of comfort in that, knowing that it's going to be a peaceful and not painful, painful end.

"One last point about death. This book provides an opportunity for you to do some political work regarding laws against euthanasia in the country of your citizenship and birth."

It's ridiculous. It's just flat out ridiculous that a person should not be able to control his own life and his own death as long as he's not interfering with anybody else's life and death. It's just ridiculous. I can't put words to it. Part of the reason I'm here in Mexico is because the US is full of rules and regulations that that prevent you from doing what was once natural.

There is a Jack London story about the old woman left out on the ice by her fellow Eskimos. It was time. That old woman probably asked to be left out on the ice, "Leave me, you guys go on. Why have to struggle to pull along an old lady when you need to be hunting for food in the winter. Just leave me here, let me enjoy a peaceful little nap that I won't wake up from." Why can't that be? It's just absurd. It's hard to even talk about it.

Lord Buckley said, "It's like the Mexican jitterbug, it's so simple it evades you."

And Milan laughed a sad laugh.

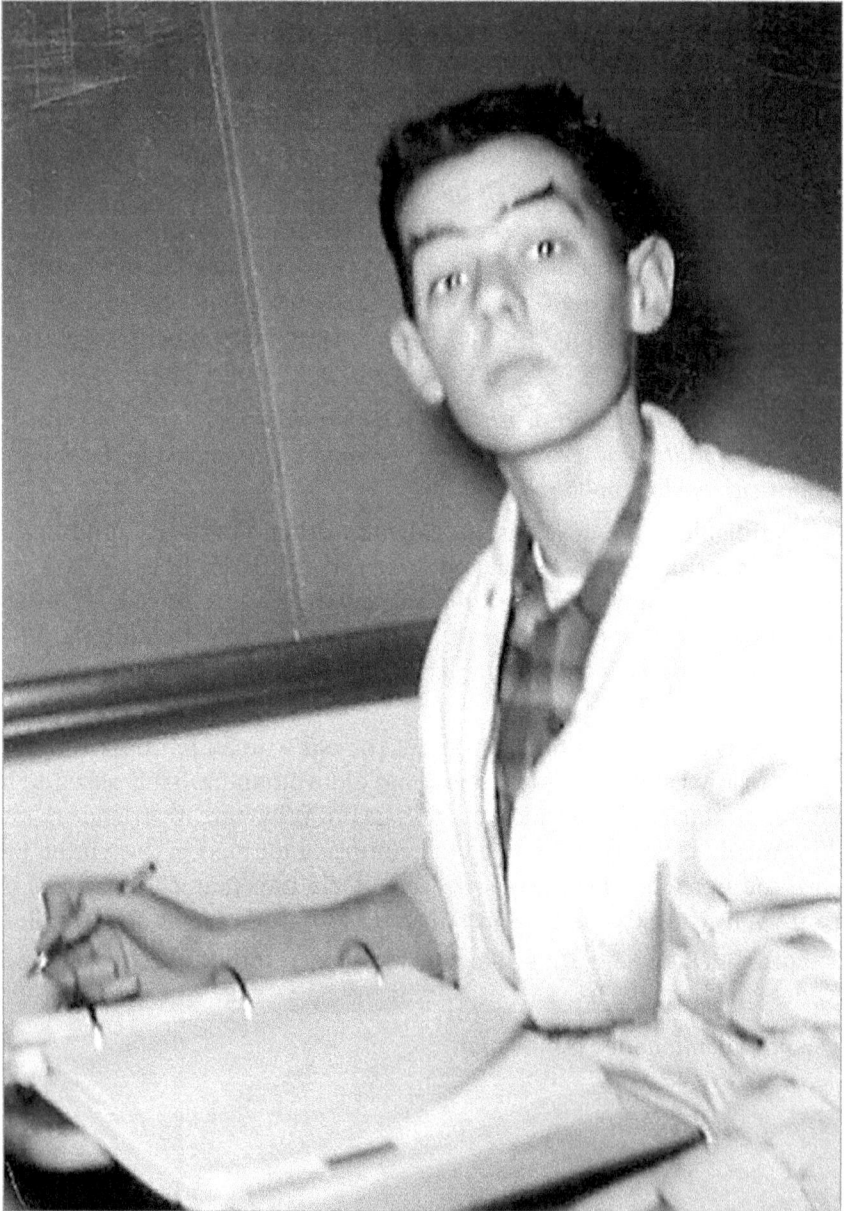

2

FROM NORWAY TO EAST OAKLAND

In the email Milan arranged to be sent out to his friends and family after he died, he referred to a possible reincarnation of himself as "the little boy in the Cowboy and Indian pajamas with the pith helmet and safari jacket." A black and white snapshot displayed on the dining table in the Puerto Vallarta apartment showed the five- or six-year-old Milan in his cowboy outfit. Milan stayed in touch with his childhood days and kept track of his ancestors.

Mocean is a Norseman, three-quarters of his great grandparents on my side of the family were born and raised in Norway. They came to the States with all of the bad habits of Norway, too. Norseman often cruised south and snatched the dark-haired Welsh beauties off the coast and took them back to put a little color into their otherwise blond and blue-eyed genetic strain. That's why both Mocean and his mother and his grandmother on my side were born with albino white hair which, by puberty, had turned to black. There is a group in Norway called the Black Norwegians that have that same trait.

But more significant to his life is the fact that the distillation of whiskey was invented by the Vikings. The distillation of whiskey was something that they took all over the world with them wherever they went. Somewhere between their raids on Scotland and Ireland and their needs to get through the long winter nights, they came up with a shorter route than fermentation and turned fermenting slop into distilled go-right-to-the-center-of-your-brain whiskey.

The term berserker also came from the Norwegians, from the Scandinavians in general. I think that alcoholic gene is something that exists in me and exists in Mocean's grandfather and his great-grandfather, and in Mocean.

On those long winter nights, when somebody just couldn't handle things anymore, when he needed to go out and club a baby seal or harpoon a whale or something, and he was stuck indoors, he would just flip out. Then his relatives and neighbors would throw his ass out into the snow and let him flip out in the snow until he realized it was better inside. But he had to get this demon out, he had to exorcise those devils, that craziness. It was accepted behavior to go berserk, to be a berserker.

My grandfather, Swen Swensen, if you can believe it, came from Norway. He was a working man. He worked for Southern Pacific Railroad for forty years. Before that he was a farmer and he owned half of Montecito in Santa Barbara. If he had held onto the land like a couple of his cousins did, our world would have been a different place than it was.

His wife and the wife of my other grandfather were maids and au pairs. They worked caring for children of other peoples' families in Germany on the way here, and then gathered in Santa Barbara with some cousins and farmed. They gradually moved north up California until they ended up in the Bay Area and that's where my grandfather worked for Southern Pacific. He helped after the San Francisco earthquake, doing what they're doing right now at the World Trade Center: dig people and things out.

The other grandmother was a strict old bird. She married my grand-father, Clarence Melvin. His grandfather, Nicholas Tack, was the first sheriff of Del Norte County, and a very stern photograph of him is in the museum in Crescent City.

I have a cousin who is a genealogist and a fanatic and who takes the family back – though there's a pretty dubious connection – to Amos Melvin. Dr. Amos Melvin cared for Paul Revere on his ride, hid him or fixed a wound or something like that, but I don't know if he's really related.

Nicholas Tack had it down. He was the sheriff and had his jail at one end of the town. And at the other end of the town he owned the saloons. He had a lock on the biz. Loggers and miners would come in from outside and get themselves fucked up and get themselves dragged down the street and put into his jail. So he did business at both ends of town.

He wed his daughter, Elizabeth, to Milan Morrell Melvin the first. Milan Morrell Melvin was an Oregon senator and lived on the land that forms the triangle between the Smith and Umpqua Rivers. These rivers run by Gardner, which was a milling town. Of course all of the logs were floated down the river and, and Milan had the idea of turning Roseburg into another Sacramento, of taking big boats containing goods that the farmers would need, and people, up the Umpqua River from Gardner to Roseburg. The Roseburg museum is packed full of Melvin stuff. The only problem with that idea is that there is a set of falls along the river between Gardner and Roseburg. But, undaunted, he had a bunch of eye-rings driven into the rocks and raised a boat up over these serious set of falls and then proceeded, during part of the year, to get a boat to Roseburg. It was a costly adventure.

He went back to the Senate, showed his colleagues what the costs were and requested funding to do it again. They denied him funding because, they said, it's not a good idea to, on a regular basis, take large boats full of merchandise up the falls.

My great grandfather said, "Well then, fuck it!" He quit and he walked out of the Senate because they wouldn't give him the money. So insanity runs deep in our family. We've got sheriffs who own saloons and senators who take huge paddlewheel boats up waterfalls.

My great grandfather Milan's wife gave birth to nine kids. These nine scattered, many of them down to California. My father was born in Oregon in what was called Marshall at that time and is now called Coos Bay. He came down to Richmond, California, to work during World War II. He was a machinist and worked for Kaiser building ships. My mother was a telephone operator.

I've always thought, I can never put this together for sure of course, but I've always thought there was a strange connection between fear and sex in my family, that they were intricately intertwined. One inspired the other, one excited the other. I thought there was fear and sex always. I got that feeling the first time when I realized I was born nine months after Pearl Harbor. I think that my folks just heard of Pearl Harbor and jumped in the sack and had a good one. I don't know.

This comes up consistently through my childhood as I discovered some of the basic facts about sex. There was always a great deal of fear involved in it. I also found fear sexy. Fear was something really interesting, real intriguing, really worth pursuing. My very first visual memory is of parties at my parent's house. A lot of the shipyard workers were there. All I remember from these parties is a hum of people in the background. But the visual memory is glasses with amber liquid. Highball glasses with cocktails in them, and beer glasses. I would go around and drink these when I thought nobody was looking. My parents would laugh at that, they thought it was a funny thing that the kid was going after the liquor.

There was so much drinking going on, it was the war, everybody was drinking. That's how you made it through the through the day and through the night I guess. You just worked your ass off all day long and a lot of people drank themselves to sleep after that. Got up and did it again the next day.

After World War II Kaiser sent its troops out to rebuild the country for industry. My father took a job in Ypsilanti, Michigan, as a machinist, renovating or expanding or building a brand new Ford plant.

We took a train across the States. But we didn't last that long, it was too damn cold, my father said. Too damn cold. He was from California and Oregon and he wasn't going to put up with that kind of weather for any reason. But they made some money, and they were brought that money back to what they thought was a good area to develop for the future: Willows, California.

My father always was in pursuit of the get-rich-quick scheme. My father had it in his head to build a roadside stand. One of those giant oranges.

At this time I'm about five years old. I remember him laying the brick himself and starting to make this restaurant. I guess the money ran out before the bricks did. They went under. They never finished it. And they had to take jobs. My mother went to work in a little plumbing store along-side the railroad tracks. Rice is grown around Willows. She worked there and she also worked at a five-and-dime store, mainly trying to keep the hobos from stealing all of the Wildwood cream oil, because it had alcohol in it. These guys would drink the hair oil. My dad went to work in the rice processing plants. It was just sheer back-breaking labor. He would come home and I would help him pick rice grains out from under his skin. He worked at the plant putting bags under the machines and sewed them and moved them and it was real difficult labor. He worked at that for long enough to get a little stake and then went to work selling. He   became, over time, sort of a Willy Loman. He was a very personable guy, told a lot of jokes, got a lot of people on his side, and was able to sell because they liked him personally. And he believed in his product.

He was selling Venetian blinds. It was a time for all of America to buy Venetian blinds. He made one-on-one in-home sales. You had to make the call, develop the client, and then you had to go into their home to close the sale. You had to do top to bottom, the whole sale. He was always selling. He liked that way better than sacking rice in the rice plant. The company developed rapidly because Venetian blinds were hot, everybody had to have Venetian blinds in 1947, 1948.

The owners sold the company and all of a sudden my dad showed up at the house one day and he said, "Well I quit."

My mom said, "You quit? Why did you quit? You were making good money."

He said, "They sold the company."

And she said, "Well, aren't they going to continue doing business?"

He said, "Yeah, but they sold the company to a couple of Jews."

My father said he wasn't going work for any Jew.

I didn't realize at the time what racial prejudice I was raised with, but as I look back now I see all of those kinds of references. I also see that we lived in an area that had no non-Caucasians other than the few Japanese who brought the rice technology to Willows. So it was pure white. I was raised in a pure white, redneck environment in Willows until the time that I was eight.

I enrolled in kindergarten. Children were red-faced, fast-moving, laughing little things who gathered in packs to tug at or make fun of my eyebrows which, at that age, dominated my face. Midway across each brow the hair suddenly swept upward to peak half way to my hairline, giving my face a distinctly devilish appearance.

I resented my eyebrows until I discovered that they served as a valuable tool – a barometer for judging the character of women, those wondrous, bright, multi-colored creatures who fascinated me to no end. Through the magic of this barometer I discovered that women fell into five distinct categories:

1) Those who admired me from afar without mentioning the eyebrows and said, "Isn't he cute?"

2) Those who gently stroked my eyebrows with open palms and dry fingers and said, "Aren't they cute?"

3) Those who wetted their thumbs and forefingers, twisted their saliva into the vertical portion of the brows in an attempt to curl them up even more and said, "I love these eyebrows"

4) Those who licked only their thumbs and attempted to flatten the peaks to conform to their own idea of normal and said to my mom, "Verna, you should fix these."

5) And one teacher in Oakland who said nothing but attempted to alter my appearance with chemicals.

When I was eight we moved down to Oakland, California. Maybe an aunt lent my father money to put a down payment on a house, I don't know why we moved to Oakland, East Oakland, and everything changed.

The rural tranquility ended. Everything changed.

Fear set in big time. I was eight years old and not everybody was white anymore. There were lots of African-Americans, a lot of Hispanics, all thrown together with us blue-collar whites. It was a cheap labor force drawn there during the War. Oakland was divided in two parts. The hills were where the rich lived and the flatlands were where we lived. I remember that being the most fearful time of my life, from 1950 to 1960. That's the time when a lot of fear was manufactured. The McCarthy era.

The nuclear scare was frightening and it's one that my father took to heart. He was always a staunch Republican. He didn't go to World War II and he always felt bad about that. He was rejected because he had massive stomach ulcers. I know he felt that he had some kind of patriotic duty to make up. His compadres had gone off and fought the war while he stayed and built ships, which he didn't consider sufficient patriotism to equal what his buddies had done.

My uncle was a Marine and one of the founding members of the John Birch Society in Oakland. He had fought in four wars, including the little, almost secret, war in China between the two World Wars.

My life was full of this fear and I was brought into discussions about things like whether we should build a bomb shelter in the backyard. Bomb shelters were something that you needed to protect yourself from the Russians and the nuclear fallout. But the bomb shelters were also something that you needed to protect you and your family from your neighbor. You had to arm yourself against your neighbor. So I remember fearing my neighbor. If there was going to be a nuclear attack the neighbor was going come take all our food and we didn't have the bomb shelter built yet, and I was just inundated with this fear, fear, fear.

These discussions at home were backed up by all of that officially sanctioned duck-and-cover propaganda in the schools during that time. We practiced the drill, duck-and-cover, duck-and-cover. Get under your desk, as if that's going to save you during a nuclear attack.

There was a TV show at the time called *I Led Three Lives*, starring Richard Carlson. It was about a guy who was working undercover for the FBI in the Communist party. I remember watching that show religiously, because if your neighbors were going to come and get your food during a nuclear attack, perhaps some of those neighbors were also Communists.

I bought into this whole right-wing paranoia and fear, that America was under attack from without and it was under attack from within also. In the middle of all this I was growing up.

In 1952, only seven years after the end of World War II, General Eisenhower was crowned king and the morals of Victoria were queen. I had just turned ten when I enlisted in the "Traffics." We met fifteen minutes before the bell each morning and afternoon, dressed in yellow jackets with white belted sashes and yellow hats, fell into formation with our stop signs on sticks mounted smartly on our shoulders like rifles. We marched in unison to our respective posts. Hup, two, three, four.

Because I was obedient, a good marcher, and displayed precision as I simultaneously took a half step to the right, whipped my open palm behind my back, and snapped out my stop sign, I quickly moved up the ranks. But not in posting. I became lieutenant by the end of the sixth grade, but Mrs. Anderson posted me in the prime location directly out front of the school's main entrance only once. Just prior to that posting she mixed up a batch of egg whites and smeared the goo across my eyebrows, hoping it would dry and hold the devilish peaks down where she knew they belonged.

As I stood at attention on the street, I recognized the approaching car of Mrs. Van de Mark, the principal. I saluted her as she braked in front of me. As I snapped my hand back down I saw her scowl and knew instantly that my eyebrows had escaped their bondage.

Mrs. Van de Mark licked her thumb.

My heart sank. What on earth could possibly be worse than wearing and smelling the old battle-ax's lipstick and saliva all day long? All my friends would know the beast had her way with me.

But she must have had second thoughts because she paused, saluted back, and then drove in. The next day I was posted to a side street.

The final humiliation of my eyebrows occurred during the year-end Traffic Patrol parade. All the grammar schools in Oakland, and there were many, sent their battalions of crossing guards to a drill competition which was judged by the chief of police, the mayor, and an admiral from the Alameda naval facility. Since I was lieutenant, I would march at the front of the ranks to the right of our captain. On this occasion Mrs. Anderson took no chances. She used Elmer's Glue.

It didn't work either. But I didn't know that until, just as we neared the reviewing stand, I saw Mrs. Anderson burst from the crowd. She slapped a pre-cut swath of Scotch tape over each eyebrow. The surprise of having this sweaty, crazed woman walking backward in front of me with the heels of her hands pressing into my eyes threw me completely out of step with the other marchers, some of whom skipped to adjust to my new cadence, some of whom did not. Suddenly, the captain shouted, "Eyes right!"

As we all snapped our heads towards the reviewing stand, we could clearly see the faces of the mayor, the chief, the Admiral, the City Council, their families, and scores of other dignitaries turn from mere boredom to active interest to repressed titters to open laughter to full-blown knee-slapping hysterics as members of our battalion skipped, tripped, slammed into each other, knocked each other's hats off, whacked one another with our signs and, in a few cases, fell to the ground.

As painful as the memory of that moment remains, I will always treasure the image of Mrs. Anderson's face. That mouth agape in a silent scream. Those eyes about to burst from their sockets. That dyed maroon hair about to be ripped from her skull by those clenched fists. How sweet the revenge when it is visited upon the enemy by themselves.

That is the last time anyone other than a lover or a wife ever touched my eyebrows without first asking.

If it had not been for early rumblings in my groin I might have tumbled to misogyny. Something instinctive told me I could not live without women in my life.

I was never sexually abused in the traditional sense, but then I was never sexually educated either, which I now believe to be a subtle form of abuse. After my sister was born in 1953, I carried a couple of dozen bubble gum cigars to school. As I was handing them out to my friends, one of them, Freddie, said, "That means they did it."

"Did what?" I inquired.

"If you got a baby sister that means your father fucked your mother."

Freddie was my friend and he was much taller than I was, but I smacked him anyway. I caught him right on his buck teeth and then jumped on him. I was not concerned for my own safety for I knew that God wanted me to take Freddie's life for uttering such blasphemy. Within seconds a crowd surrounded us. Everyone had heard the reason for the fight, and those who knew the score, sexually, rooted for Freddie. Those who did not rooted for me. Unfortunately for the sexual health and safety of America, most were on my side. As Mrs. Anderson kicked her way between us with those blunt semi-high heels, I knew we would be taken to the principal's office. I gave up the onslaught because I knew I would find my revenge in the person of Mrs. Van de Mark. She would know the truth, punish Freddie for lying, and I would be the school hero, perhaps getting a better crosswalk posting.

Midway down the hall I got my first inkling that something was amiss. Mrs. Anderson let go of Freddie's collar and started violently shaking mine. She yelled something about "Traffics shouldn't behave like that!" which really confused me because I felt sure that Traffics were future defenders of motherhood, God, and the nation.

Mrs. Van de Mark did not help clarify the situation. She told Freddie he had used a very poor choice of words and dismissed him with only one detention. She told me I should not start fights, no matter what anyone said to me, and she gave me five detentions. Now I was really baffled. Women, the power structure in my school, were protecting some deep, dark secret from me. That secret had something to do with sex. I vowed to discover and expose that secret. Thus began my lifelong fascination with espionage.

With the help of various radio-serial and breakfast-cereal code rings I studied cryptography, and with the help of an older neighbor kid, Perry, who owned a crystal set, I studied radiography, and, recognizing espionage's most valuable tool – women – I studied them in their larval stage: girls.

I encoded several notes and passed them to select female subjects. The missives contained the frequencies of certain radio stations (Perry had developed a technique that he said would allow us to override a station's signal for a few blocks radius and replace it with our own) and the time when we planned to broadcast. After a song like Rosemary Clooney's "Come-on-a-my-house, my-house-a-come-on. Come-on-a-my-house I'm-a-give-a-you-everything" finished playing on the chosen station, Perry, whose voice had already changed, would say something like "What is 'everything'? If we come to your house what are you going to give us?"

At school the next day I would ask the girls the same question. Some responded with, "Cookies and milk, like the song says," and others would say, "Nothing! Because you're not coming to my house." I reported my findings back to Perry, and though we talked about it for hours, we got no closer to unearthing the female secret.

My big break came one afternoon in the late spring of 1954. We were given the entire afternoon to play sports. But a few minutes into the first game of tetherball, I became suspicious. There was not a woman or a woman-to-be anywhere in sight. Clearly they were all in a secret meeting somewhere. I faked an emergency toilet need and walked from the yard into the building holding my stomach. I continued down the empty halls past the Boys room and ducked into the Traffics locker room. It adjoined a room adjacent to the entrance to the back of the stage in the main auditorium. I tiptoed up onto the stage and hid behind a curtain.

A slide show was in progress. As I peeked out I saw the faces of every female student and teacher in the reflected light of the screen. In order to see the projected image I crawled down stage, hugging the darkness of the wings.

There, in all its black and white, grainy glory stood a cross-section of the world's largest vagina.

I didn't know it was a vagina at the time, but I was overwhelmed nonetheless. At first I thought it was a drawing of the mushroom cloud that follows a nuclear explosion, but then I realized it was blueprints of a military operation. The school nurse, the same woman who taught us to duck-and-cover under our desks during a nuclear attack, stood before the screen pointing with a long stick at various fortifications within the enemy camp. Her voice-over confirmed my suspicions.

"Cells build up on the walls of the uterus and if the ovum is not impregnated that material moves down through this passage. This phenomenon is known as menstruation." There was talk of spermatozoon but no mention of penises. It made no sense at all. I stayed until the end, but I still didn't have a clue. I reported back to my friends; they didn't either.

I would have to resort to my last option: questioning my father.

I asked him point blank, "What's the girl's big secret?"

He thought for a moment, said something about guessing it was time I knew and then proceeded to divulge all he would ever say to me on the subject of sex. "If you get blue balls, masturbate. Go somewhere and do it right away, even if you have to duck behind a billboard. Rock aches aren't good for your later years."

Clearly this was a technique he had developed on his own. He was raised by three older sisters, the youngest of whom was ten years older, and who I doubt ever knew much about the procedure. But I trusted the man at the time and spent my teen years trying to pound down those uncontrollable boners that seemed to pop up several times a day.

One of my favorite diversions during junior high school was down by the Chevy plant on 73rd Street. I lived on 82nd. On certain days of the week the train that transported Chevy parts from the Chevy plant in San Leandro to the Chevy plant in Oakland ran past the house at a time that was convenient to hop on board and ride the train to junior high, which I always thought was a hoot there in Oakland.

In junior high there was more paranoia. The McCarthy period was in full swing. A lot of teachers bought into it. Communists everywhere. Then in '57, I started Castlemont High School. I was a tall, skinny, shy kid and I don't know how I ever became student body president. I felt I was sort of like molded, that I was handled in some sort of manner because I didn't really lust for the power, nor did I see the power or any point in it. It wasn't an attractive thing to me. But I was elected senior class president. The fraternities discovered me and I was brought into a fraternity called The Shamrocks. That's when the fear and the sex really got going. I didn't have wheels so I was always in the back seat.

I basically was destined for the straight Republican life.

Before I knew it, it was the late Fifties. Ike was still our national hero and leader, though J. Edgar Hoover controlled more than we will ever know, Nixon could not have been "a crook" because he was vice president, John Foster Dulles and his brother, Allen, were creating the western world in their own image, and Khrushchev vowed to bury it. Joseph McCarthy had come and gone but the House Un-American Activities Committee was still turning people's lives inside out. Communists were everywhere. In the sky, in the movies, and in Cuba. After *I Love Lucy* the most popular show on TV was *I Led Three Lives*.

The good news, though, was that Queen Victoria's influence was fading with each of Elvis' undulations and all of Big Joe Turner's shakes, rattles and rolls.

Personally, I was torn between patriotism and pulling my pud, trapped in a life or death struggle between idealism and onanism.

If the Communists were under every bed, they would certainly be on to me. They might blackmail me. Get me to give up some student council secrets or something. The Reds must have followed me, my friends and our girls as we parked on dark lanes in the hills above East Oakland. Commie spies were reporting back to Russia what we would not admit to ourselves: American youth was committing crimes against the Code of The Queen behind those steamed-up car windows.

Lots of us, too. There were traffic jams on otherwise unused roads until at least midnight on weekend nights. It was almost impossible to find a place to park. We all seemed to arrive at about the same time and left at exactly the same time. We huddled together for the safety in numbers. We had all heard of the White Witch whose daughter had been raped on this lane. She still stalked the night and would murder both boy and girl if she caught them parked alone. And that guy with the hook! He was out there somewhere with a new hook. His last one was discovered hanging from somebody's older brother's Chevy door handle, and The Hook Man was mad enough to kill.

I didn't have a car in high school but I managed to get in the backseat with my girl, Suzanne, each weekend. It was always a strange moment when, in the middle of some hot and heavy petting and panting, the first car engine would start up. Had the Witch struck? Was the guy scraping his hook across someone's steamy window? No one took the time to find out. We all turned our engines over and peeled out; no wanted to be last.

And so it was, with one hand on my heart and the other in my pants, I joined the Federal Bureau of Investigation as an undercover informant.

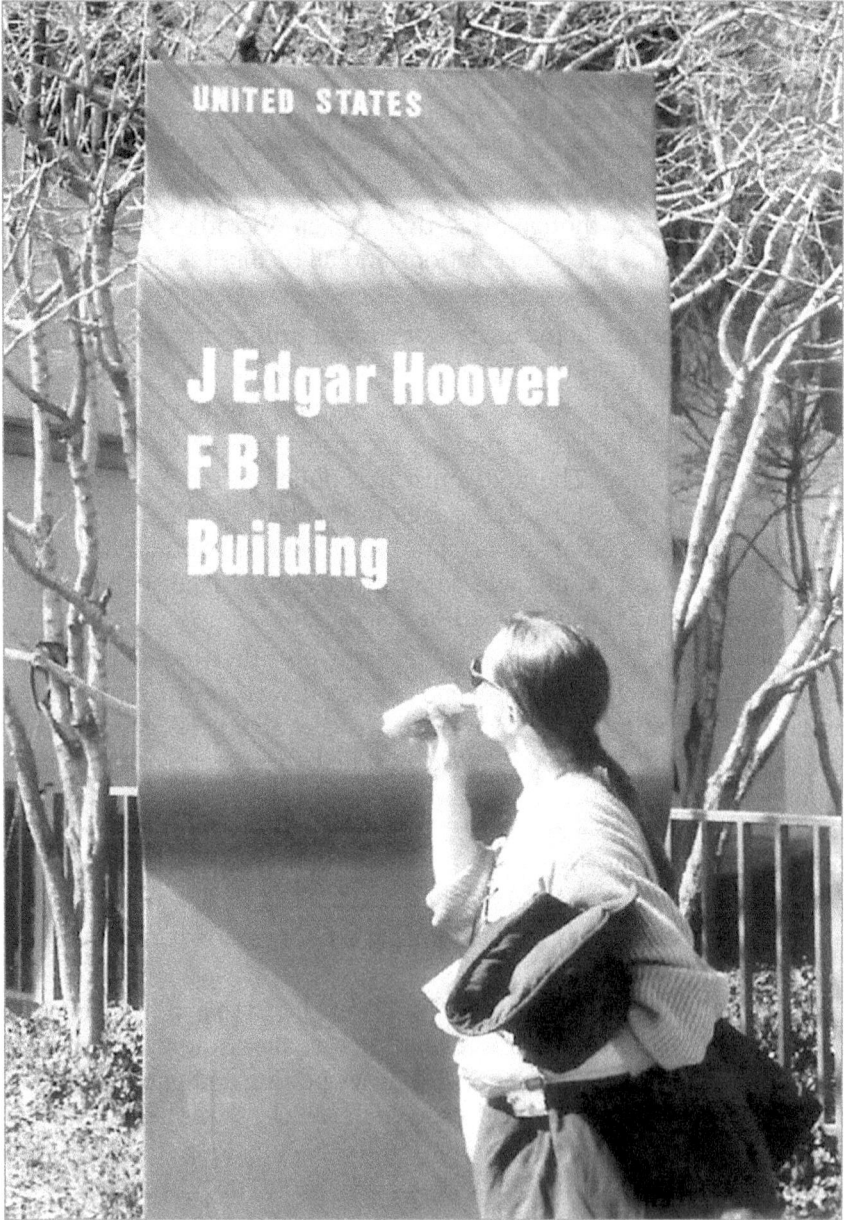

3

Working for the FBI

Over the years since the late Sixties, Milan has told and retold the story of his FBI years to a wide variety of audiences. He told it one more time to me in Puerto Vallarta.

I enrolled in the University of California at Berkeley in 1960. At the time there was a big discussion in my family, headed by my John Bircher uncle, who was asking me basically why I had chosen that little red house as my college. Couldn't I have done something better with myself?

I chose Berkeley because it was a good school and because it was cheap and it was close.

I remember my uncle and my father insisting that I join the Masonic Club, so I would be at least in touch with some sane elements out there, where all the rest of the students were Commies. At least I would have this refuge alongside the campus, the Masonic Club, where I could go be with kindred souls.

The fact of the matter is, and I know I've obscured this myself, but I don't know to this day – I mean I don't remember – if I was recruited or if I volunteered to work with the FBI on an undercover basis. Somehow this FBI agent came to the Berkeley Masonic Club. That's where we met. We talked about a career for me with the FBI.

This discussion about becoming a FBI agent turned into what I could do now to combat this menace that he and my uncle and my father were so worried about. And what I could do now was just keep my ears and eyes open on campus for the enemy.

The FBI agent said that he knew I didn't have a lot of money, somehow he had background on me, they'd done their homework. He said they could help me with some of the money needs that I had, and with tuition. He also knew I had dental problems. I had a lot of dental work that needed to be done. He told me there was a dentist who was very cooperative with them and that this dentist would help me for free.

Suddenly two big problems, money and money for the dentist, disappeared for me.

Pretty soon we started talking about what exactly I would do for them for this assignment. He said there were some public rallies I could attend and maybe later tell them if I knew any of the people at those rallies.

That's how it started. They informed me of public rallies going on and sent me to them and then afterwards we would meet. They would pick me up on a different corner each time. I learned some of the tricks of the trade as far as making sure that you're not followed, the basics of surveillance and counter-surveillance. We would meet – there usually were two of them – and I would sit in the back of the car and study photos they brought and say, "Yes, I saw this guy."

All of these rallies were already covered from top and bottom by these FBI photographers. It was a training ritual to break me in, to get me used to this pattern of identifying photographs and telling them what I knew.

Next I was asked to get close to certain people. They knew there was a class that this one guy Doug would be taking, so they asked me to take that class and try to become friends with him. They started moving me in. They got me jobs, summer jobs and after-school jobs. One job was proofreading diplomas. There was a guy proofreading diplomas they wanted me to get to know. Another job was spooling wire. They gradually moved me into the circle of the Communist party.

I asked Milan if he was troubled at all by this work at the time or if he believed he was just doing his patriotic duty while picking up some needed cash.

I was a zealot. I was driven. I bought the whole program, the whole patriotic program. The money and the dental work were relieving. But the money was almost an insult in the beginning; however they made sure that it was always part of the deal and they made sure that it always increased.

I kept saying, "It's not worth this money, I don't want to be doing this for this money."

And they said, "No, no, no. We know that and we just want to make sure that you have more time. You know this little bit of extra money can buy you a little bit of extra time to do the kind of work that we know you want to do."

So it was zealotry. It wasn't the money that drove me to this.

Did you share this at all with your flag-waving uncle and father?

Yeah, and they were both just super proud. Just super proud. It was a way that I could make up for my father not having served in the military during the war. It was a way I could continue the service of my uncle. It was a way I could really take what they'd done and carry on, do so much more.

I was thrilled. I was loving it. I was very satisfied with what I was doing. And then I moved into this social circle and actually became the roommate of one of the principals I was assigned to follow. He was the son of one of the honchos of the Communist party there in Berkeley.

He was a good guy. That's the thing that began to turn me against the FBI. The circle of friends that I met through Doug were really good people. Really interesting people. Far more interesting than the people I was seeing in my parents' neighborhood back home. They had fun at their parties. They laughed a lot more. It was just a more interesting set of people. That was the first thing that began to install a little guilt in me about what I was doing.

But I continued. It was my work. It was what I agreed to do.

You continued to do this with a sense of guilt developing, developing a friendship with this fellow and his friends?

And his friends, yeah. And they gradually began to be my friends.

I was learning about jazz and I was learning about folk music. That turned me on to the whole folk club scene. It was these people that turned me on to the things that I still enjoy most today.

What were you telling the FBI at this point about your new friends and their activities?

It was just answers. I volunteered no information, it was just answers to their questions. It would always be based on photographs. Who is this guy? How long has he been here? Of course a lot of the people I didn't know because they just came off the street to rallies.

The turning point for me was when I was asked to start organizing rallies and forming groups to inform on.

They wanted you to become a provocateur?

Yes, the provocateur, exactly. I was creating the problem, or we as the FBI were creating the problem that we were investigating. The idea was bait to attract subversives. They asked me to form a group called Youth for Jobs, in Oakland and Berkeley. I did, and we got a couple of rallies off the ground, and I ended up on television a couple of times. I was basically asking for more jobs for young people.

The main turning point for me was a speech that they had me organize with Gus Hall, the head of the Communist party, in 1962. That's when and where it became clear to me I was working the wrong side. They had me organize the rally and invite the people, they photographed the people, and then I identified the people.

I thought to myself, wait a second, "I'm not here for what I thought I was going be here for. I thought I was going to be doing something to help my country. I don't see how I'm helping my country. I see only that I'm setting people up and building a case and evidence against them."

This was J. Edgar Hoover's COINTELPRO weirdness.

How did you come to that conclusion? Did you think that through on your own or did you discuss that with friends and family?

I thought that through alone. There was very little I could discuss with anybody about this.

When you told the FBI, what was their response?

I never really challenged them. I never told them my conclusion. John Le Carré, who writes great spy novels, put his finger right on the button about what spying is all about. It's really not for the money and it's not for the patriotism: it's for the control that you have. You're in the driver's seat. You're the only person who knows what you know. You can play all the world off against itself because you're the only holder of that information. You can divulge part of it, all of it or none of it to one side and vice versa. I think I became enamored with the game of spying. I stayed in it a little longer than I was comfortable, for a total of, I don't know, two or two and a half years.

I was slowly already living another lifestyle, and the FBI didn't like it. By then I'd met Chan and a lot of people in the folk clubs and had an apartment on my own and was dealing marijuana in the alley behind the Cabale coffee shop in Berkeley. Still, because of the control I had over these guys, and because of this pretty substantial money they were giving me at the time, I was cooperating to a degree. But the degree was very slight. I wasn't telling them the whole stories. I participated less. I lied about events that I'd attended. I just wasn't their guy anymore and they knew it.

Do you think you compromised anyone during that period?

Oh, I don't think I ever told them anything they didn't already know. I think I was, at best, corroboration. In 1966, or at the end of 1965, they came to me, they tracked me down in Reno and they asked me to testify. They were going to launch a case against the SDS and bring them up before a grand jury as a Communist front group. I was their star witness, or at least that's what the FBI agent who came out from Washington told me. He said J. Edgar Hoover personally had dispatched him to see me.

Not only did I decline to testify, but I declined in a way that was pretty harsh. I bet you can find that letter in my files. It was a way that made it very clear that I wasn't in any mood to cooperate with them in any way.

While you were figuring out your exit you were giving them less information, and you were not giving them straight information, and you were selling marijuana and hanging out in music clubs in Berkeley, how did you finally sever the tie?

Swede came to me, my contact. I believe his real name is Everett Nelson. My contact name was Nick Nickles. Every document I signed was signed Nick Nickles. It wasn't signed Milan Melvin. Every document, every photograph, everything I ever touched was signed by Nick Nickles.

Swede said to me, "I know what you're up to. I know what you're doing."

I said, "Then why don't you just leave me alone?"

He pleaded with me in his avuncular way. He was a good guy. It was his wife who later phoned me, not that damn long ago, in the last several years anyway, to say that Swede really felt like I was his son. He wasn't a bad guy. He never appeared like a bad guy to me. He was always a very avuncular figure, always trying to help.

He pleaded with me, he said, "No, please, you have got to straighten out your life."

We had a couple more meetings like that where he tried to talk sense into me, and I basically disappeared on him.

By that point a pal and I bought a bunch of parts in a box and we put together three motorcycles. And I got a Harley '74 out of it. I'd already been up to Nevada a bunch of times. So I just took off. I left the apartment and much of what I owned and took off up to Nevada. This was in 1963.

I hid in the desert and surrounded myself with friends up in Silver City and the Native American Church and the folk music and marijuana culture.

I had discovered through people like Chan, through the Cabale coffee house, this connection to Nevada. Nevada offered the exact opposite of Berkeley. Berkeley was dark and clandestine and everything seemed to be hidden and juggling two, three worlds at a time. Nevada was the exact opposite. It was wide open. It was daylight. It was desert. It was freedom. There was nothing in shadows. There was the whole American Indian experience that Nevada offered. I discovered the freedom and the openness of Nevada. It was such a breath of fresh air, literally and figuratively, to be able to escape to Nevada and be with friends who were living around the Zen Mine scene and the Native American Church.

Some of your friends and colleagues suggest that there was no cut-off date in your federal funding, that, on the contrary, the locales that you've slipped into and out of worldwide correspond to your continuing employment with the federal government.

No, that's not true. I've only discovered in the last couple of years that rumor about my continued involvement. Somehow in the story my employment got switched from the FBI to the CIA. However, that rumor of my continued involvement with the clandestine world has helped me out, helped me avoid some of the assholes. It's a great asshole filter. Most of the people I know and love – like you – have no fear of hanging out with me. Those people who do fear it are people who I don't want to hang out with anyway. I haven't really cultivated that rumor. I've been surprised a couple of times when people have come out nowhere and made off-the-wall accusations about my still being a CIA agent.

Has your work for the FBI been a moral burden to you over the years?

Well, I've always been forthcoming about it, which is probably what's added to spreading the rumors. I came out on the radio in San Francisco. I've always said, "Look, let's have a little compassion for those who haven't realized yet what's going on. And let's realize that anybody can change. That anybody can be on the wrong side of an issue, figure it out and come on over." That's the nature of humans, which nobody has figured out a hundred percent and anybody can start anywhere and get over to where they should be on any particular issue. I've always been forthcoming about it and that's been good and it's been bad. I mean it's helped me and it's has hurt me.

At the same time as he came out on the radio, Milan wrote this letter to his draft board.

San Francisco, California, July 24, 1969

Local Board No. 52
Selective Service System
2030 Franklin Street
Oakland, California

Gentlemen:

I have returned my Selective Service Registration Card and Classification Card to your board. This is my statement of reasons why I have made such a move and I would like it to become a permanent part of my Selective Service record.

Let me start at the beginning of the process which led me to this decision. I graduated from high school in June of 1960 and enrolled in the University of California at Berkeley in September. The University was commonly referred to as the "Red Beachhead" and the "Little Red School House," especially by my fellow members of the University Masonic Club. I felt it my patriotic duty to help rid the campus of the subversive elements which had given the University such an image. So in the fall of 1960 I contacted the Federal Bureau of Investigation in Oakland and volunteered my services as an undercover agent. I was met at the Masonic Club by Everett Nelson of the Oakland office and we discussed how this might be done; other FBI agents that I worked with were Bill Weisskirk and Don Jones.

I was employed as a salaried undercover agent for the FBI for almost three years, during which time I joined and informed on several "subversive" people and organizations, such as the W.E.B. Du Bois Club, the Young Socialist Alliance, the Progressive Labor Party, and several minor "front groups" like Youth for Jobs. I was a full-time "member" of the Communist Part for over a year – all the while serving dutifully as an undercover agent.

During these three years of dual involvement with United States Government Agencies and the groups on which I was spying I came to the realization that the names and claims of rampant subversion were based on fear and not fact. Among the thirty thousand students on the University campus, there were only fourteen members of the Communist Party – hardly a "Red Beachhead!" More important was the fact that these so-called "front groups" such as Youth for Jobs really were more concerned with getting employment for people of the ghettos than with recruiting members to the Communist Party – this came to be a more meaningful project and honorable life style than sneaking reports to disguised agents and feeding the fear of international espionage.

In no way did my work as an undercover agent advance the cause of freedom, justice and equality for the people of the world; it only set it back that much farther. I will forever be ashamed of the damage done to the personal lives of those whose names I turned in – every undercover agent tends to exaggerate in his reports in an attempt to get a little more money each month – even though my reports were only a few more pages in an already stuffed and useless dossier. However, I am now able to speak from a position of experience in both factions; I would not be where I am now if it hadn't been for this double life.

I believe that the Communist Party is as guilty of a need to gain power as the United States Government is guilty of maintaining power. I see no difference between the neo-Czars of Russia and the Nixons and Lairds of this country; each waves missiles at each other in the name of "World Peace"... somehow they miss the point.

Peace will not be achieved by violence; the means you use will dictate your end result. The recorded history of mankind will bear this out – thousands of armies have been formed to rid themselves of oppressors, only to become those oppressors, e.g. the Bolsheviks after the Russian Revolution and the United States after the Second World War. Violence begets oppression and more violence.

Peace of mind will never be attained while we fear attack, imprisonment or subversion.

Peace on this planet, or any other, will happen only when all men live as they want all men to live. I believe mankind does want peace, happiness and confidence; but most individuals are afraid to make the first move, each clings to his rifle hoping everyone else will drop theirs first. By returning my draft cards to you, I think I have made my first step – I will no longer consider myself a member of organized violence. If all men refused to participate in organized violence, there would none... "Suppose They Gave a War and Nobody Came." The conditions of this world will not change by putting different faces in the same seats of power – it will change only when men change and each man has to start with himself.

If this act results in a jail term for me, I will consider it an honor to feel free and honest with my own conscience within the walls of your prison. History will not convict me of some crime that the German officers were convicted for at Nuremberg – I am not following orders, anybody's orders.

I ask you Gentlemen: Is there no some higher meaning of life than to protect yourself from other men, some more profound reason for living than to have as your occupation the operation of a Selective Service System? What exactly is the service that this system selects men and boys for – is it not the perpetuation of fear, "self-protection" and mistrust among men?

Sincerely,

Milan Morrell Melvin

In Puerto Vallarta, he told me he felt quite secure that his FBI work caused no harm.

I didn't name names. In 1965, when J. Edgar Hoover sent that agent to Reno to track me down because I registered at the University of Nevada, to tell me that I was going to be the star witness against the SDS, I refused. It's bothered me, yes. I've been guilt-ridden behind it. But when I look at it, when I get logical instead of emotional, I realize I didn't do anything other than experience a period of transformation for me. I actually did something heroic, I think. I followed my heart, then I realized that what I was doing was wrong, and I stopped. That shouldn't bear any guilt. That should be just what it is.

Did that change of heart adversely affect your relationship with your father and your uncle?

Yeah, because gradually the signs started to show. I started to grow hair and my dress started to change and I showed up on Harley Davidsons. Yes, there was a great deal of friction. At one point during this period my uncle offered me his sword. For a thirty-year Marine to offer his sword to someone is about as important on the honor front as a move as can be. I refused that sword. I told him that I no longer agreed with him and with what our country was doing and I was actually ashamed of having done some of the things that I'd done. That was a big family upset.

In the mid-1990s, while living in Wolf Creek, Oregon, Milan began writing his autobiography. He finished fragments before putting the project on hold, most of which appear in some form here. He based the book proposal on a visit he received from the FBI after making a Freedom of Information Act request for his files. Since the FBI did not provide him with the background, he wrote a report on his encounter with the FBI agents who came to his house to check on his request for his file and followed that report with his own variation of what could have been in their dossier.

"Hello."

"Is this Milan Melvin?"

"Who's calling?"

"I'd like to speak to Mr. Melvin personally."

"Then you'll have to tell me who's calling."

"Special Agent Michael Conroy, Federal Bureau of Investigation, Eugene Office."

FUCK! You brought it on yourself, pal. Now take a deep breath and answer the man.

"Mr. Melvin?"

"Yes, this is Milan."

"We just received a communiqué from our headquarters in Washington, which we'd like to discuss with you personally. Is that possible?"

"When?"

"How long does it take to get from Eugene to your place?"

"About 45 minutes."

"How's 45 minutes from now?"

"No, later, uh two o'clock."

"Two is fine. Let me see if we've got the right address."

He had it right.

At two on the button, he and fellow Special Agent Carl Swanson roll down my driveway in a nondescript brown four-wheel-drive Bronco and park alongside the house. Through the curtain of an upstairs window I watch them open and peer into a file between them; there is an 8 x 10 glossy and a couple of typewritten sheets within. They close the file, get out of the car, and approach the front porch empty-handed. I meet them there, we exchange names, they flop out their badges and photo ID. We shake hands. I lead them inside and introduce them to my wife, Georgeanne. They decline her offer of coffee and she slips out of the room with a line about "cookies in the oven." She never bakes cookies, but there's something about two FBI agents on one's couch that makes one want to appear wholesome in all aspects and act domestic in the extreme. I got into the spirit, too.

"So, how's business?" I ask.

"Fine," Conroy replies.

"How was the drive down?"

"Very pleasant, very nice day."

Enough already.

"So, what's up?" I blurt.

"Well, Mr. Melvin," Conroy again, "in a nutshell, we've been asked by our main office in DC to verify a couple of things with you. Headquarters wants to make sure that it was you who requested your files under the Freedom of Information Act and to be assured that you were under no coercion to do so."

"Yes and no. Yes, I did ask for my files and no, no one is forcing me to do so."

"Thank you. That's it really."

An awkward pause ensues during which Georgeanne who, cookies or no cookies, has not been out of earshot, suddenly joins us and sits on the arm of my chair. Both our faces must read: You drove all the way out here to ask that? But Conroy wants to change the subject, get chummy.

"So how do you like living in Wolf Creek?"

"Love it, but listen, back to my files. What's going on? I sent requests to San Francisco and Washington over nine months ago. San Francisco reported back that they had nothing on me and I know that's bullshit because I wrote for that file. I used to work undercover for you guys, 1960 until sometime in 1962 at UC Berkeley. I was a Communist for the FBI, just like the movie title. I wrote scores of reports. My code name was..."

Both agents protest, hands up, palms out, and try not to profane the sacrosanct by actually allowing the code name to enter their ears. From Conroy, "No, no, you don't have to tell us that." Swanson shakes his head in silence. He's been silent since he passed on the coffee.

I go on, "You know the deal. You report who was at a meeting and include your own name so no one with access to the report can figure out who the mole is by process of elimination."

"Then you sign the code name," says Conroy, "and no one knows it but the agent you're working with. I know, I used to do what you did at the University of Miami, but ten years later, during the anti-war movement."

"So why is San Francisco saying they have nothing in their files about me?"

Agent Conroy: "Honestly, we don't know. We only got this request to come see you this morning."

Finally, Agent Swanson: "If something does exist, what would you do with it?"

Bingo! The real question they came to ask.

I give them the real answer. "I want to find out if my father initiated my recruitment or if it was something I did on my own. I was eighteen when I started with the FBI. My son's eighteen now and when I look at how politically naive that age group is, I realize how I must have been putty in someone else's hands. I want to know whose hands. It's written somewhere in your files. I want to see it."

"Really, we're completely in the dark about any files on you," said Special Agent Conroy. "But, I can tell you this, I've been an agent for twenty-four years and I've never been asked to perform an assignment like this. You must have some files back there in DC!"

As I watched the two agents drive away I realized that they must have had some portion of those files right there in their vehicle because they had not asked me for any photo ID. They had my photo with them in that file in their car and needed only to see my face to verify my identity.

It's been over a year now since that visit, two years since my original request, and I've received nothing from the Feds, probably never will. But if I were to receive the files and if they weren't ninety-five percent blacked out "for reasons of national security," the outline might well serve as chapter headings, something like:

Background checks on Milan Melvin revealed an 18-year-old Caucasian born in Richmond, California, in September 1942 to a telephone operator and her husband, a logger-merchant marine-machinist-turned-salesman and member of the Masonic Order.

M. Melvin was recruited from the Masonic Club at UC Berkeley and formally trained by his case officer in the fall of 1960 and entered left-wing politics as an undercover operative at the behest of our agency. He remained in our employ for almost two years, during which time he penetrated the young Communist movement on campus, at times acting as an agent provocateur at our urging.

In 1962 he began to falsify his reports, omitting the names of certain left-wing activists whom he seemed to have befriended. When confronted with these facts by his case officer, M. Melvin responded that he had had "pangs of conscience," had acquired a "new point of view politically" and resigned, effective immediately, stating that he felt himself to have become a "left-wing radical."

Closely monitored by our agency for the next year, he experimented with drugs, married in a gospel ceremony, rebuilt motorcycles, then dropped out of college and all political involvement. Immediately after being re-approached by his case officer, he dropped out of sight, apparently crisscrossing the country disguised as an American Indian jewelry trader and member of the Native American Church.

In 1964 we attempted to apprehend him on charges of marijuana importation from Mexico. We pursued him across five states but never captured him.

In the summer of 1965 M. Melvin surfaced in Virginia City, Nevada, at an establishment called the Red Dog Saloon and was initiated as a member of a Hell's Angels-sanctioned motorcycle gang.

In January of 1966 the Justice Department planned to prosecute the Students for a Democratic Society for subversive activities. J. Edgar Hoover personally dispatched one of our agents to inform Melvin that he would soon be subpoenaed to testify against certain SDS members and offered a deal wherein records of his criminal activity and all charges against him would be expunged if he cooperated. In a direct written response to Mr. Hoover, Melvin wrote that he "would rather be known as a faggot than an informer."

In 1967 he started "underground radio" stations in San Francisco and Los Angeles with Tom Donahue, produced music recordings (Blue Cheer, Screamin' Jay Hawkins and others) and consorted with Janis Joplin. A year later he married Mimi Farina, singer, anti-Vietnam War activist, and sister of Joan Baez, who wrote a song, "Sweet Sir Galahad," about him.

In 1969 Melvin came out of his "clandestine closet" by publicly declaring himself a former FBI operative who was against the war in Vietnam, and, in spite of entreaties by his former FBI handlers, took his draft card to the Selective Service Board, tore it up and instructed the desk clerk to "tell Hoover to put it where the sun don't shine."

Because of his on- and off-screen role in a Warner Brothers film, the company flew Melvin and his Harley Davidson to England in 1970. He is known to have lived in Paris, then ridden to and lived in the south of Morocco until 1971, when he and his motorcycle were flown back to Los Angeles by United Artists for another film, which was cancelled shortly thereafter. He rode his motorcycle from LA to New Orleans, sold it, flew back to Paris, met actor Sterling Hayden (a reluctant but cooperative witness for the House Un-American Activities Committee), then returned to America with him and attempted to co-write a screenplay.

Except for a few brief visits, he remained out of America for almost a decade. According to US Consular officials in Kathmandu, Nepal, M. Melvin received a 90-day visa to stay in Nepal but remained for over four years by bribing Nepalese immigration officials. He is known to have snuck past Gurkha army checkpoints into restricted territory along the Nepal-Tibet border in the high Himalayas in order to live and travel with Tibetan Khampa guerrillas. He also formed a trekking guide service to fund construction of a day-care center for Tibetan refugee children in Nepal.

In December 1974 he and his wife slipped into Laos. Then while trying to escape across the Mekong River back into Thailand, they were captured and detained by a unit of the CIA's clandestine Meo guerrilla army as it disassembled a heroin refining factory.

For four years beginning in 1976 he traded and smuggled gems out of India, Burma, China, and Hong Kong, manufactured jewelry in Thailand

With Howard Hesseman on Saturday Night Live

and sailed the South China Sea on a Chinese junk with his wife and new-born son, eventually settling in Bali, Indonesia.

In 1980 Melvin assisted film director Carl Gottlieb in Mexico during the filming of United Artists' motion picture *Caveman* with Ringo Starr, Dennis Quaid, Shelley Long and Oakland Raider John "The Tooz" Matuszak. Shortly thereafter Melvin managed the entertainment career of Matuszak.

Our next direct contact with Mr. Melvin was in 1981. He was producer of a television show but also appeared to be at the center of a money-laundering operation involving 24-karat gold jewelry from Thailand. We interrogated him on tape under oath in his home in Los Angeles but could not charge him with any clear-cut crime.

In 1982 and 1983, Melvin accompanied actor Howard Hesseman to New York for his two appearances on *Saturday Night Live*, one time riding Hesseman out of an elevator on a Harley Davidson and on another occasion participating in a sketch during which he carried a large poster-sized photo of President Ronald Reagan onto stage that Hesseman proceeded to "moon," inviting the nationwide viewing audience to join him.

According to the Drug Enforcement Agency and a Federal attorney in Seattle in 1985, Melvin was the target of a grand jury investigation that suspected him of being the man known as "The Professor," a multi-ton, multi-shipment smuggler of marijuana from South America and Southeast Asia. No indictment was sought due to lack of evidence.

In 1988 Melvin traveled to the Soviet Union as part of the ABC television company that filmed *Head of the Class*. On two occasions he was reported inside the US Marine guard compound on the grounds of the US Embassy in Moscow in the company of Hesseman, other cast members and boxer Mike Tyson.

For three years beginning in 1989, Melvin and his wife, Georgeanne, co-owners of a women's apparel manufacturing company, raised and funneled hundreds of thousands of dollars' worth of medical and material aid to an organization called CoMadres (the Committee of Mothers of the Disappeared) and other antigovernment organizations in El Salvador. On two occasions during the civil war they personally delivered the aid and are thought to have been in the company of FMLN guerrillas.

Larry Hankin, Carl Gottlieb, Ed Begley Jr., David Crosby and Milan.

Until recently Melvin lived with his wife in seclusion in Wolf Creek, Oregon, where Special Agents M. Conroy and C. Swanson visited them after he requested copies of his FBI files. Melvin was elected Worthy Master of the local Grange, his wife held the position of the Goddess Pomona, and together they led a successful campaign against toxic waste incineration.

4

NEVADA: PEYOTE, INDIAN TRADING
AND THE RED DOG SALOON

It was to fill in the gaps in his autobiographical manuscript that Milan and I were talking in Puerto Vallarta. We were working from a yellow legal pad on which he had carefully identified the missing adventures. Next on the list was Nevada and the Native American Church, trading with Indians, and the Red Dog Saloon.

I disappeared into Nevada and discovered the Native American Church. I remember Chan taking me to my first peyote meeting. They packed us full of peyote and treated us to a full-blown American Indian Native American Church ritual from dusk to dawn. I know nobody came out of that meeting the same as they went into that teepee. We city-oriented, city-raised people connected with the earth, and there was no turning us back ever. We came out of that somehow a combination of cowboy and Indian. We came to know Mother Earth. We came to know that there was another way of living other than scrambling in our own little self-made ghettos in the city, and very few who attended that meeting ever went back to the city. We all headed across America.

I didn't understand what it was at first. It didn't start until nighttime and it was in a canyon that nobody could find. We stumbled around, it was like some bizarre initiation rites for some goofy Elks Club or something. We stumbled all over the goddamn desert, for what seemed like half the night until we finally arrived at this teepee that was aglow with fire. We walked inside and man, it was like going back four centuries. Inside there were all these grinning people and the warmth of the fire and the drums beating and the smell of the cedar and I knew I was home. I knew I didn't have the double life to lead anymore. I knew I didn't have the city smells to ooze in to my body. I knew I was home.

I spent several weeks wandering around Nevada, trying to figure out how I could make a living there. I mean I've always lived by the creed that one should go to where one wants to be and then figure out a way to support oneself to stay there. That's what Nevada was like at that time for me.

The only way that I could figure out to do that was to start smuggling marijuana up from Mexico. That's when, with various pals, I started going down to Mexico and buying a kilo or two at a time and bringing them up to Berkeley or San Francisco and selling them and then just coming up to Nevada and spending the rest of the time kicking back.

There was so much to discover in Nevada. There were all these abandoned mine shafts and luscious junk sculptures lying all around the desert from the old mining times. It was virtually frozen after the Comstock silver rush. Frozen in time for a century. It was just such fun to walk around. I disappeared into the desert except for these runs down to Mexico to buy a kilo or twelve and strap them under the car and drive back across the border.

The old trick in Mexico used to be that the guy who sold you the weed would turn you in to the border guards. Then he would get his weed back and a little reward. The border guard would get his gold star for having caught somebody.

On one of my runs I was concerned that this trick was being used on me so I devised a game to figure out if I had been reported to the border guards. I bought maybe ten kilos of weed that was loose and I just crammed it, just stuffed into a backpack. Then I rented a motel room on the Mexican side of the Nogales border. I left the backpack in the motel room and went up and crossed the border to see if I or my car had been reported and would be stopped and searched.

I pulled up to the border and this American customs guy said to me, "What country were you born in?"

I said, "The States."

He said, "Okay. Go ahead."

Obviously I had not been reported. So I circled back around into Mexico. I went back to the hotel and threw the backpack full of loose weed into the trunk and got my cowboy hat. That was going to be my excuse when I got up the border the second time. I was going to tell them that I had forgot my hat, so I went back to get it.

I pull up at the border and there's been a shift change. There's a new guard.

The new guard said to me, "Pull over there into the inspection area."

I pull into the inspection area and now I'm starting to get worried. Just as if he knows exactly what was going on, he said, "Get out of the car please and open the trunk."

The trunk was where I'd thrown the big knapsack full the weed. So I walk back with knees beginning to shiver and open the trunk and he reaches right in, and grabs the knapsack full of weed and is about to open it when I said, "Be very careful with that. That contains ten-million-year-old paleoanthropology slides."

The guard very gently put the bag down. He said, "Oh, I'm very, very sorry. I'm sorry." He gently shut the trunk and said, "You can go now."

I got about twenty minutes outside of Nogales on the way to Tucson when the excitement overtook me and I simultaneously lost control of the car and pissed my pants and crashed into a yucca tree. So I vowed to try and come up with some more sophisticated measures than muling it myself in the future.

Were you ever busted?

No. Never busted.

Were you ever concerned about any ethical or moral questions regarding smuggling?

No, no, not at all. Actually it was a revolutionary act at that point. I couldn't see any reason why marijuana should be illegal and I decided that as long as it was illegal, it provided a chance to make a buck.

I simultaneously was campaigning for it to be legal.

There are so many stories about successful and failed attempts at smuggling. Poor Chandler one time put the weed his tires, inside the tubeless tires just south of the border. He was going to drive across the border and take it right back out so that the pressure and the heat didn't affect the weed. After he crossed he thought he was being followed. He didn't take it out of the tires until he reached Inverness, up in Marin County. At that point, when he did take it out, it was all this hot, rubbery weird goo. I think Chandler was able to sell it off as Malaysian opium or something.

I remember when the run from Berkeley to Nevada was getting known to the authorities. The Highway Patrol started looking out for longhairs or people dressed like beatniks. I remember Chandler was always a lot laxer than I was on security. We were headed up to Nevada one time and we had this crumpled brown paper bag with about a half a pound in it, which is sizable. Half a football.

"Ah, Chandler," I said, "Chandler, like we've got to tuck this away somewhere, man."

And he said, "No, no, it'll be all right. We'll be okay."

I said, "No, man, you know we've really got to tuck this away. Got to hide it somewhere."

He said, "Well, if they decide to search they'll search, you know? Then they're going find out where we're going put it."

There was no arguing with him. Somewhere above Sacramento, somewhere around Auburn, sure enough, the Highway Patrol pulled us over and there was this bag of weed.

I watched Chandler, as if by magic, make the obvious invisible. The Highway Patrolman told us to open the door and said, "Why don't you fellows just stand over there to the side?"

I did immediately and he started to search the seats, started to feel down between the front seat, back, and the bottom. There was this half a pound of weed in the crumpled brown paper bag right where the guy is about to put his hand on it.

Chan said, "Here, I'll get this out of your way." And he threw it over into the back seat while the cop searched the front.

Then the cop went to the back seat and started to grab the bag and Chandler said, "That damn thing again. I'll get that out of your way."

He kept moving this thing and I just kept watching this half a pound of weed move all around the car. He tucked it in above the sun visor. He put it in the glove compartment box, he took it out of the glove compartment box. He put it under the seat, he pulled it out from under the seat. It was just the funniest thing I've ever seen. Eventually the guy let us go.

There is another famous story about Chandler that's changed over the years. Everybody who's told it has elaborated on it. Chan used to have this big full-ton International pickup truck with a steel I-beam welded on the front as a bumper. Impregnable. He was on the Embarcadero Freeway one time when the Highway Patrol pulled up alongside of him and saw him finishing a joint. The Highway Patrol frantically waved him to pull over onto the side of the Embarcadero. Chandler said yeah, he'd do that as soon as he finished this joint.

The cop in a much more frail car than Chandler's couldn't force him over like they might have if it were a regular sedan. Chandler took his few puffs and then swallowed the joint or threw it out the window.

When the cop pulled him over, Chandler no longer had the joint that the cop saw him smoking, which was the reason for pulling him over.

The cop said to Chandler, "Where's that joint?"

Chan said, "It's gone."

The cop said, "Do you have anymore?"

Chandler said, "Nope, that was it."

The cop looks onto the seat and he sees the little brass container, not much bigger than a postage stamp. The cop reaches in, he grabs it, he opens it up, and there's some residue down in the bottom.

He said, "You don't have any more, huh? Well, what's this?"

Chandler bends over and looks down into the little brass container and blows into it hard and said, "Nothing."

The cop was twice foiled. He was pissed. He spins Chan around and throws his hands down across the hood of the vehicle and is about to handcuff him and sets down the brass container. It still has a little residue in it, enough, if the cop wanted to be a stickler, to bust Chan. The cop reaches back to grab his handcuffs, at which point Chan, with one hand free, reaches up, grabs the brass container and throws it off the overpass. The cop thrice defeated now flips and starts just whaling on Chan, kicking at him and punching at him. When backup arrived they found Chan under his pickup truck defending himself with his feet with this cop wildly frothing at the mouth and kicking at Chan. I think they arrested them both.

The appeal of the outlaw approach was to have fun. As Dylan said in his song, "To live outside the law you must be honest."

I found it a very honest lifestyle. One where you could live what you truly believed in and not just live by the laws that existed, laws that often were in conflict with what I believed. I think the reason I got into the FBI in the first place was because I believed what I was told in grammar school about freedom and the importance of it. The things I learned in grammar school, the things many of us in our generation learned about liberty and freedom of speech, we learned from the Constitution. We believed them and we wanted to really live them. Not live them in quotes.

One should always have the right to free speech. That means a hundred percent, not just free speech unless you have extenuating circumstances. That's what the outlaw life was about: living honestly, and getting back to some of the basics of human life, many of which are boldly and clearly and honestly and poetically stated in the Bill of Rights and the Constitution.

But it's got to be fun, man, because if there's no fun there's no reason.

The Native American Church was fraught with male chauvinism. Their rituals are very male-oriented and males have all the power, even though the Earth Mother is the one in the morning who brings nourishment and life and rebirth to everybody. The men run the meeting.

There's the roadman and that roadman has a staff and a rattle with him. He sits directly opposite the door at the back of the teepee, the doors always faced east, to the rising sun. There's a crescent, the road of life. The crescent sits before him molded of sand or clay or dirt.

To the left of the roadman sits the cedarman, who is in charge of purifying the air and the elements and the people within the meeting. His instrument is cedar shavings and cedar leaves. When someone enters the tepee, the cedarman always sends cedar smoke his way to clarify him and cleanse him of the outside elements that he's brought back in with him.

To the right of the roadman is the drummer. The drummer keeps beat with the rattle of the roadman.

By the door is the fireman, and he's in charge of keeping the fire stoked but under control all night long. At the end of the night, or about three o'clock in the morning, after the sack of peyote has gone around two times, the fireman lets the fire die down to embers, still hot, but down to embers, and these embers then are shaped by the fireman into a peyote bird. By the time he finishes shaping them it's pretty dark inside the tepee.

At this point the roadman asks all in attendance to mount their prayers, to put their prayers on the back of that peyote bird. That peyote bird, if we do it right, if we all put our energy into it, can fly out of the smoke hole in the top of the tepee and carry those prayers up into the cosmos, up into the heavens to Father Sky.

I've see it happen only a couple of times, but I've seen people put all of their energy into that bird on the floor, all of their prayers, the reason that they are there at that meeting, the thing they came to ask for, all put onto the back of that bird, and then the fireman starts to fan those embers with his feathers. Everybody who has a feather in the tepee, also begins to fan those embers. That bird materializes out of the blackness, out of the dark embers, onto the floor, materializes and begins to turn red, and then finally turns white hot and lifts off the floor. I've seen all the Indians together lifting their feathers up to the sky and fanning that bird right on out of the top of the tepee. It's an amazing event. The real deal when that happens.

The fifth officer is a woman, the Earth Mother, who is in charge of water, sending water around, and in charge also of the seven dishes that are brought in in the morning.

Stuck in the two poles on either side of the door are what are called pee sticks. These pee sticks are often beaded and flowered and brightly decorated and are used to control the entrance and exit of people. No more than two people can go out at a time, that means that you must carry a pee stick with you.

The point is that no matter how loaded you get on peyote – you're standing outside there with your dick in one hand and the pee stick in the other hand and the sky's full of stars and the snow is reflecting all the diamonds of the earth and all the wonders and the rocks and the moon and the shadows and the clouds, and everything is just about as psychedelic as it could possibly get – eventually your musing comes back around to this pee stick and that's your connection. You're reminded to get back to the meeting. That's your connection psychically to what's been going on in the meeting, but it's also your reminder to get back to the meeting. Eventually you work your way back and turn the pee stick over to somebody else and then, upon your entrance, the cedarman again cleanses you with the cedar smoke, cedar and sage.

Women were never allowed to beat the drum in the most traditional of the circles. It's only the men could make the prayers and the women were there to support them. This chauvinism perpetuated these males as cowboys, women as squaws role models for us for a while which, of course, didn't help the feminist movement much.

We were living like wild cowboys and Indians. We had to improvise. One of our tools was using drive-away cars. Somebody moved to the East Coast and wanted their Lincoln or their Cadillac or their Mercedes delivered to the East Coast. They flew there and wanted their car driven there. It paid about fifty dollars plus gas and you got this very expensive car to drive to the East Coast.

At that time abalone shells were not considered of much value by anybody except the Pueblo Indians in New Mexico. We would go with these brand new Cadillacs or Lincolns to Morro Bay and fill them with abalone shells, which stunk to high heaven. We tried to protect the cars as best we could with plastic bags, but we actually stunk up the cars pretty thoroughly.

We filled up these cars with free abalone shells and then we would drive them to New Mexico and trade the shells to the Pueblo Indians who made *hishi* or some other kind of jewelry out of them. In return for these abalone shells they traded us turquoise jewelry. We then continued to drive at very high speeds with the windows down to New York, and sold the turquoise jewelry for enough for a plane ticket to fly back and do it again. That was one of the ways that we supported ourselves.

All this time that I'm racing around, the FBI is still trying to get a handle on me. They've got a renegade agent out there basically, who's run amuck. I know they're trying to keep tabs on me. I'm moving as fast as I can, about as fast and as hard and as low and as off the radar as you possibly can. But they were trying. They would pop up every now and then.

This concern shows up in a letter home that Milan wrote at the time:

I am trying to avoid returning to Berkeley – *he wrote to his mother, father, and sister* – because of the hassles I would have to go through while attending school. I got much, much too involved with people I don't want to be around anymore. Here in Denver I can stay at arm's length from everyone. There are no phone calls, no more people asking me on the street to carry picket signs or to help organized demonstrations. Many people I met are involved in things that I want no part of. It is hard to say these things to you folks because I know you want me to be near. I have found a different way of life. I love it. For the first time I feel free. There is room in Colorado, New Mexico and Arizona to stretch my arms wide. A man can make a mistake here and no one else cares. I've met new and beautiful people here that I can learn many things from. The biggest question in my mind is whether or not I can live in Berkeley as I choose to live here. I picked up my mail this morning and found my "Happy, Happy Birthday" cards. It sure was nice, thank you.

Love,

Milan

Milan didn't share everything that was happening in Denver in that letter home.

One time Chan and I were hanging out in Denver. I had a little sandal and leather business there and I don't know what he was doing. Chandler and I were hanging with this Indian guy, half Apache and half New York-born street hustler. This half Apache had a whole line of pottery and one night we went over to his place and we saw him wildly packing up all of his pottery equipment because he heard that there was going be a raid. We went down to the coffee house and we heard, yeah, sure enough, the FBI was on the way to raid him because he was using underage out-of-state teenagers to polish his pottery. Chandler and I barely made it out of town in front of this raid on this place. I suspect that they also had yours truly as one of the targets.

Chandler and I left Denver, made it as far as Colorado Springs, where the Air Force academy is located. Chan had a big "Fuck Communism" sign in the back of his pickup truck. He and I were starving and burst into this pizza parlor. It was Friday night and all the cadets were there for pizza. We were the only guys in there without white sidewall hairdos. By this time our hair had grown pretty long and we were looking pretty, pretty wild for 1964. Vietnam was beginning to pick up and we were obviously not fodder for that war. We were against it.

Even before we got our pizza we realized that we probably should split. Murmurings were beginning. Guys were pointing. Guys started shouting. Then some guys started to throw stuff at us. Chandler and I went out into the alley to get in the pickup truck. Come bursting out of this pizza parlor, there must have been fifteen of these guys all shouting at us and fists doubled up. Some of them carrying I don't know what to smack us with. It was Chan and me with our backs to the pickup truck and these fifteen guys charging down the alley. We reached into the pickup truck and grabbed whatever weapons we could. I got a tire iron and Chandler found a machete. We started to charge back in the other direction when my guardian angel – who is a short statured African American guardian angel about eighty years old, mostly bald, little tufts of white hair and little white moustache, little white goatee – came by on a bicycle. He rode between the two camps and said to me with his little toothless – yes, my guardian angel has no teeth in front – said to us in this little toothless whisper, "Police, police."

Chandler and I realized right around the corner were the police coming up. We were standing there with machetes and tire irons in our hands, it wasn't going to look too good. We didn't want to get booked. We put the weapons back in the truck, the cops rounded the corner and saw immediately the two of us standing there like innocent angels as these fifteen guys charged down on us to beat the crap out of us. The cops interceded to save our lives and escorted us to the edge of town, instead of locking us up. This was when the Fed-gars were on our trail pretty tight.

The Fed-gars?

The Fed-gars. The FBI.

I've never heard that term.

Edgar! J. Edgar Hoover!

Chandler and I disappeared. We got out of Dodge on that one. We kept one pace ahead of the Fed-gars down into New Mexico into Taos and Santa Fe, and then west, across Utah and Nevada and eventually up over one of the Yosemite passes to come down into California the back way.

Chandler went to hide in Inverness and I went to ground all the way over in Hawaii.

Just over some half-Apache using under-aged pottery polishers?

There was a pot-dealing scene also. They must have had half a dozen or two dozen different charges and they were going to make a sweep. They did sweep, they did get a bunch of other people for other things, but they didn't get us.

I made it over to Hawaii and landed, I went as far as I could in Hawaii, to Sunset Beach, which was only thirteen cabins. I landed with a bunch of other outlaws, birds of a feather attracting one another. Twelve of the cabins were occupied by military personnel from the various bases over there. All of them had re-upped two or three or four times because it was the only way they could stay out of jail. They went home and stole somebody's pickup truck or punched somebody in the mouth or broke into a liquor store at night or robbed some place because somebody wouldn't sell them liquor at four in the morning or some damn thing. And the local sheriff offered them the option to re-up or to do jail time. So they re-upped. They were dyed-in-the-wool thieves and each of them worked some place where they would organize a heist.

Somebody would call one night and say, "Okay, bring the pickup truck and those crates." We'd load up the pickup truck and the crates and we'd go to Hickam Air Force Base and somebody'd just received like ten million dozen eggs. They peeled off two hundred dozen eggs for us. The next time it would be shoes. The next time it would be canned hams. But the hams never came at the same time with the eggs, so always you were long in one thing and short in everything else.

They were all inside jobs at the military bases. The crowning event for that was when somebody said bring the pickup truck and the tarp. They had baked a brownie that was six feet long by four feet wide; it was for the troops the next day. We took the whole Goddamned brownie. Twenty-four square feet of brownie that we had lashed to the top of this pickup truck and threw the tarp over it. We all had brownies forever.

They were just dyed-in-the-wool thieves who had to steal and figured out that surpluses were easy marks and nobody would notice it.

That was 1965, when Chandler was putting together the Old Red Dog Saloon. Ah, the Red Dog Saloon.

The Red Dog Saloon was a bar and music hall in Virginia City, Nevada... and a state of mind. Milan was a founder.

The Red Dog experience really began on the highways on the way up to Virginia City, Highway 50 or Highway 80. Sacramento seemed to be the gateway to the Red Dog experience. As soon as you hit Sacramento and passed it, you realized that the Sierras and the Comstock were ahead of you and that's where everybody broke out their stashes and began the Red Dog experience.

The Red Dog, to me, was an outlaw enclave. It was revolutionaries, outlaws and hustlers, hookers, go-go dancers, anarchists and beatniks and musicians and Indians. You know, quality people! People you could trust at that time.

If one word comes to mind to encapsulate the Red Dog experience and the people who were there and the way we felt about one another, I think trust is that word. I know that if I need to get underground or get help, or whatever, as long as we know that one another is out there, we're all okay. We've all spread out all over the country, so it's good that the underground network stays intact and that the outlaw enclave, although it's spread out, is still supportive and in touch and able to receive anybody who goes a little bit too far over the line at any time.

The music was what it was all about, I think. The music was so good I collapsed. I don't know if it was the altitude or the good drugs or what. But I danced myself into a frenzy, passed out flat on the floor, and had to be carried to the hospital. The Charlatans were playing my favorite song, 32-20. The Red Dog was originally conceived as a venue where we could dance, so the music was the center of it. The Charlatans, the house band, were perfect for the place.

The Fifties was a time when those who were hip were driven indoors. It was a nighttime scene, it was a jazz club scene, it was a beatnik scene. We nodded our heads in dark clubs to jazz music and the drug of choice at the time was heroin. There was a lot of pot smoking, but there was a lot of nodding also going on.

That was true of the early Sixties also, I think, until the drugs of choice became the psychedelics. Psychedelics forced us outdoors because there was the beauty of nature to enjoy, and Nevada has about as much nature as is possible.

Nevada's seasons are violent and wild, its earth is everywhere. The clouds in the Nevada sky don't fool around with little projects. They are massive, sweeping clouds that go in all directions. In Nevada you can see for scores of miles. Getting everybody up to the Red Dog was getting everybody out of the Bay Area and out of those dark clubs and into the outdoors.

That's why our Nevada became such a wild, outlaw experience, with people wearing pistols and popping them off at American Flats. I think it was a reaction to that whole darkness of the Fifties.

Was an overriding philosophy developing for you at this point or were you just careening around and things were just happening?

I'm careening around and things are just happening. I thought about art at that time. I thought about the commitment that one must do to become an artist and about the possibility of going crazy if one commits oneself entirely to one art. There's the possibility that one will be driven crazy by that art. If you don't make it, if you don't achieve what your own goals are for yourself, you've set yourself up for a major disappointment, and disappointment in the extreme means madness. So there began to creep the realization that my life is my art, that I'm having such a good time and living in a way that people seem to find interesting, that the careening becomes the end goal in itself. The journey is the destination.

Milan and Mimi Farina

5

THE WIVES AND JANIS JOPLIN

"And the women... " Chan wrote in a good-bye email to Milan, musing about the old times.

I'm a serial monogamist. I like relationships that are solid. I don't like running around. And I don't like the dating scene. I prefer to be married with one person and settled in with one person. It's kind of like traveling. I'm a terrible tourist but I'm a great live-abroad. I like to go places and get into them. I like to connect with a woman, with a mate, and really get into that one relationship and not maintain the dating scene. I'm a terrible dater.

I did, in fact, stand at some kind of improvised altar five times. The first was with a woman named Sheri Williams and it was in a gospel church, a couple blocks down from the Cabale on San Pablo in Berkeley. We were the only white people at the ceremony. The minister married us and we took off to Nevada for a honeymoon in a Volkswagen bus. That lasted about eight months because we went back to Florida and met her father. He was a very rich cat and I think he told his daughter, "Look, lose him or lose your inheritance." She divorced me.

The second marriage was to a woman named Zella.

Zella who?

Zella Morton, I think, I can't remember. She was a dancehall girl. She was a dancer at the Peppermint Tree in San Francisco. I snatched her off that stage and brought her up to The Red Dog Saloon in 1965 and she was the star attraction, other than Lynn Hughes. Zella basically taught Nevada how to dance. That lasted a year or so. In the middle of our marriage the FBI swooped in on me and wanted me to testify and I said no. I went through a lot of changes behind that and that was part of what broke up our marriage.

Then in 1968 I met and married Mimi Farina. Mimi and I were married two, two-and-a-half years. Her sister Joan wrote a song about us called "Sweet Sir Galahad." At the time I felt it was a song I couldn't live up to. We got married in the worst year of my life, 1968, the year Martin Luther King was assassinated, the year that Bobby Kennedy was assassinated, the year of the terrible Tet Offensive in Vietnam, and many other terrible events. It was just hard to maintain the relationship, especially one so wound up in political activism. She was an active anti-war figure and I was becoming one as a result of my involvement with the radio station. In 1968 I came out publicly on the radio as having been a former FBI employee who was against the war in Vietnam.

You had to make a statement in '68. You had to come out and do something and a lot of people were trying to evade or avoid the draft, but I wanted to make a statement that I just wasn't going. I took my draft card, my Selective Service card, down to the Selective Service office and turned it into them and said I didn't want to be any part of this war effort and I was refusing to go. They looked at my 1Y status and looked me up and found out right there on the spot that I was politically untouchable. The FBI had given me this 1Y status so that I would not be drafted and there wasn't in fact any danger of my being drafted.

But I still felt I had to make a statement. I had to say publicly that I was former FBI and that I was not going to participate in this war in any way.

I wrote it as a letter to my co-workers at KMPX.

Mimi and I were married at the Big Sur Folk Festival, which was quite the hippie wedding.

Crosby, Stills, Nash and Young performed together for the first time at our wedding. It was great to have them and people like Joanie Baez and Joni Mitchell and John Sebastian and a lot of other people from the folk scene singing at our wedding. I left that marriage with Mimi in August of 1970, when I rolled out of town with the Medicine Ball caravan.

In 1972 I was living comfortably in Nepal and Bonnie Bales showed up. She was a stewardess for United Airlines. I had met her once or twice swimming naked in Tom Donahue's pool in Mill Valley. Tom gave her my address and she tracked me down in Nepal and said without any ceremony whatsoever that if the two of us got married she could give me ninety-percent discounts on airplane tickets. I could accompany her anywhere in the world.

Being the guy who loved to travel, that was an impossible offer to turn down. Tom Donahue married us at the radio station in October 1972. We stayed married for seven years and had our son, Mocean. In 1979 we broke up. Mocean stayed with me.

From 1980 to 1982 I lived with a young woman I didn't marry, which was amazing. But I lived with her monogamously: Gigi. I married when I should have dated, but in this one case I did date and live in.

In 1982 I married Georgeanne Edgar. That marriage lasted eighteen years.

Do you want to make any further comment on these women, or do you want to just list them?

No, just list them.

But in the boxes of his material that Milan directed me to sift through for this project I found the email correspondence between him and author Alice Echols, research she was conducting for her book on Janis Joplin.

She and I certainly gave each other all we craved sexually – *Milan wrote to Echols in 1997 about his relationship with Janis* – but, out of the sack, I was not willing to Velcro myself to her side while she dealt with the backstage madness or the personal problems created by making up and breaking up with her bands.

When I tumbled for Mimi, there was no formal breakup with Janis because there was no formal relationship. We just had a fuckin' good time, that's all. Only after the initial rush of settling in with Mimi did I realize my feelings for Janis ran much deeper than I recognized, but I don't really know how Janis took it. She never said.

I remember rumblings ranging from "That son of a bitch!" to "Milan who?" We were not monogamous. We had other lovers. She was in and out of town. We would call each other and connect or not, then move on with or without each other. And, of course, it was the Sixties. We were free-lovin' all over the human map, having more fun than we deserved, often avoiding commitment and keeping things loose in case something exciting appeared on the horizon.

At one point I wanted to get back with Janis, even when I was still with Mimi. I missed the excitement, the abandon, the going for it all that Mimi and I never shared. But when I did see Janis next, there was a chasm of sadness between us that we couldn't cross. I don't know if this had anything to do with our own relationship or with the tremendous changes she was going through with her professional life. She never said. She just stood there near tears. Me, too. All I could do was stomp on that Harley and get in the wind.

The last time I saw her it was at her Mill Valley house. I told her I really loved her last album and she responded that she did too. Finally, she said, she felt she was able to sing, really sing, not just shout. As long as we stayed on music, she was exuberant. That must have been May or June of 1970, and that's why I know she didn't commit suicide. There was too much joy, too much confidence, too much future, too much fun to be had with her music. She was only getting started and said, "Wait until you hear the new tunes" she was working on. Then the subject played out and there was nothing else to say.

We found ourselves on opposite sides of the pool table, staring at each other silently until the sadness in her eyes became unbearable. I said I had to go and she said she had to rehearse and we were both lying, but all I could figure to do was jump back on my scooter and get the fuck outta there.

First thing that attracted me to Janis was her laugh. We were all raised in the Fifties with its oppressive Victorian/Christian morality and good girls of that time were taught not to laugh out loud. Only bad girls threw their heads back and belted out a laugh like that. Janis was definitely a bad girl and I loved her for it. Our generation loved her for it. After the bad taste left in our mouth from the Fifties, we needed a bad girl.

I can't remember how I met Janis. I just remember Janis and me coming together like crazed wildcats in heat, just kicking and clawing and biting and scratching and making love to one another until we were near dead and then getting up and taking some more drugs and then doing it again. But I do not remember anyone saying, "Milan, this is Janis."

She could move tens of thousands of people like they had never been moved before but she was so vulnerable, so easily hurt. Her highs were higher, her lows were lower. For her it was a very short distance between joy and devastation. She desperately wanted to succeed, to be accepted by a mass audience, but she hated the business of rock 'n' roll. The money meant nothing to her compared to her music.

The last time I felt her was after her death when I was in Paris. She wrapped her arms around me, pressed her cheek against my back, squeezed me tight and then she was gone. And so was I.

Milan defined his relationship not just with Janis, but also with the drugs the two of them shared.

Both fame and heroin attract lowlifes. Especially the latter. Every cliché about junkies is true to some degree: liars, cheats and thieves. They will steal shit off their grandmother's – or anybody else's – bureau to trade for a fix, if they're strung out and too broke to cop. A junkie is anyone who ever tried opiates and liked it. Once you realize that, it's only a matter of defining one's habit.

(Fortunately, I've got mine down to a nice little run every ten years or so. According to my calendar and, especially in the light of all this conversation, it is time! Even more fortunately, I'm flying to Asia in a few days and I know somewhere out there is just the right wispy-bearded old Chinese cat to fix up – say – a week's worth of pipes... then I'm good, probably till the next millennium.)

In the piles of papers Milan left was a scrap with a simple map showing directions to Mr. Fung's Opium Den in an alley off Bo Bazaar Street. It's marked as in the apartment house (4th floor, apt. 14 by stairs) in the alley between shacks and buildings. This must be a referral because the handwriting does not appear to be Milan's: "My friend John has been at Mr. Fung's for two years smoking opium. They make good pipes here, a conservative Chinese den, soft voices, easy movements, free Chinese tea."

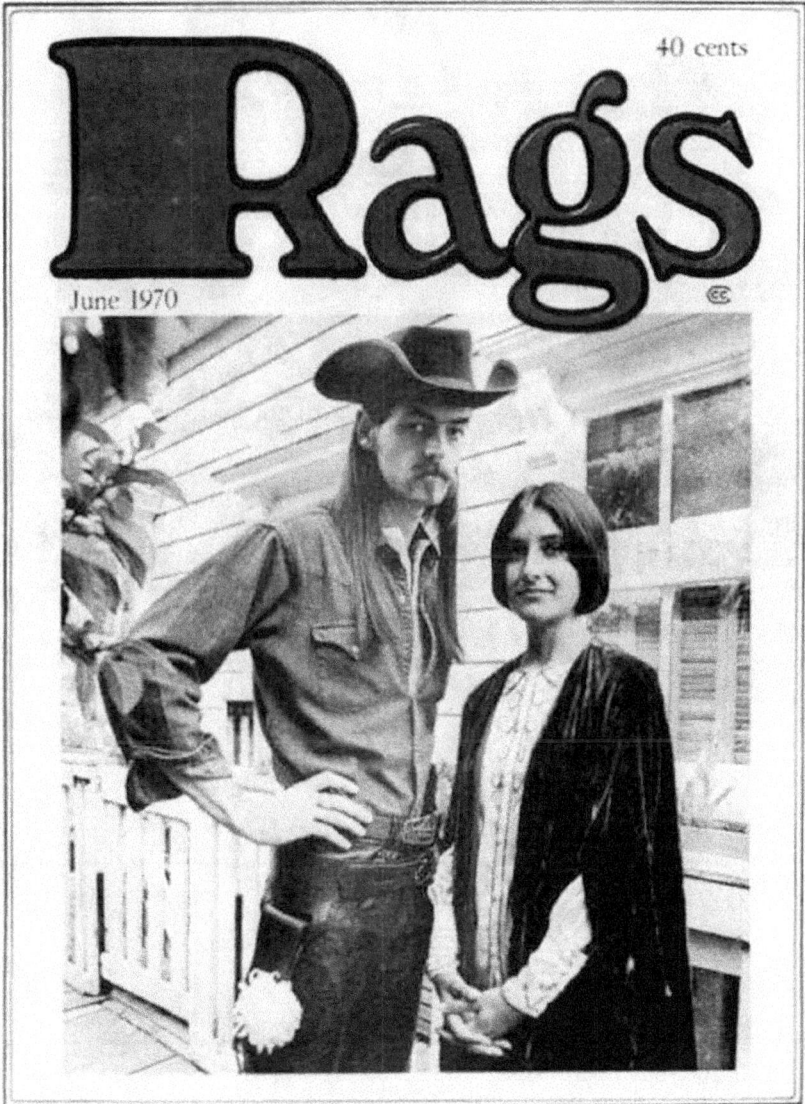

40 cents

Rags

June 1970

The KSAN crew

6

Inventing Underground Radio

On to Milan's radio career.

What a thrill to hear underground radio for the first time. Given the state of Top 40 radio at the time, underground radio was nothing short of revolutionary.

I remember the night clearly: spring 1967, North Beach, San Francisco. My roommate, Carl Gottlieb, a member of The Committee, heard backstage that a new radio station was on the air, a station for "us," whatever that meant. He rolled the FM dial to 98.6, KMPX, cranked up the volume and what I heard changed my life.

Rumbling out of the speakers was a voice like no other, a deep basso profundo that made my teeth chatter and rattled glassware all over the flat. But the voice wasn't shouting like the Top 40 jocks, it spoke in tones unmistakably mellowed by marijuana, like it came from a friend sharing the same bench in Golden Gate Park. And when the voice stopped, the music started, not a two-minute thirty-second single with a repeating hook, but an ethereal twelve-minute instrumental, a raga by Ravi Shankar, segued seamlessly into a gospel choir then blended into BB King, and followed by a long Rolling Stones track. The regulation pimple cream commercial never materialized. In fact, no commercials aired.

It was in stereo, amazing on its own for the day. Carl and I couldn't believe our ears. Three hours and six joints later I knew I needed to get in on this action.

The next afternoon, I met the man to match the voice, Tom Donahue, damn near four hundred pounds of him. I told Donahue point blank that I wanted on the team: on the air, in the record library, on the wastepaper baskets, in the lobby, anywhere, any kind of a foot in the door.

Tom replied with a few financial realities at KMPX. The station was deeply in debt and getting closer to bankruptcy by the day. He joked that the way he found KMPX was to call all the radio stations in the phone book until he got to one whose phone had been disconnected; he knew then that he could get this station to try his concept of programming. He was working for free, he told me, and if I wanted to volunteer to work on the same basis I could choose just about any position I wanted. Not on the air just yet, he added, because he held the 6 pm to midnight slot, Larry Miller (who had been on for a few months before Tom) occupied the midnight to 6 am spot, and the rest of the day was handled by Bob Postel, the 24-hour a day, 7-day a week engineer.

Bob was a pale, skinny little cat who existed solely on coffee and the odd chicken sandwich. He was responsible for playing the tapes submitted to him by a variety of religious and foreign language groups whose programming went from 6 am until Tom came back on at 6 pm The religious and foreign stuff produced very little income for the owner, Leon Crosby, so we reasoned that the best thing I could do for this new sound was to generate some money. That meant hit the streets, sell some advertising, buy out the foreign programming, and make ourselves a 24-hour sound. In short, take over the joint.

Anxious to start immediately, I asked Tom for a rate card. He laughed. He hadn't gotten that far yet. (I realized at this juncture that this was below ground-floor entry level; this was somewhere down in the magma.) We made up some rates, some very flexible rates. Tom wanted some ads on the air, if for no reason other than to chum the waters, to give other potential advertisers a taste of what they could expect. If I couldn't sell any ads immediately, I should trade out a few, especially to restaurants, so Bob Postel could get a little something to eat.

In these first few days I couldn't even give away advertising! Reason? Almost no one could hear us; damn few of our potential clients could get our signal. If your receiver wasn't in North Beach or if you were in the signal's shadow behind one of San Francisco's many hills, you where shit out of luck. And so was I.

Most retail businesses, like the head shops I targeted, had AM/FM receivers with a heretofore unused FM band in their shop, but when I went in and tried to tune it to our station, I usually got only static and amused looks from the owners.

Back to the drawing board.

Tom got technical help, probably from Bob Postel and Paul Boucher, an engineer who was still at KYA, Tom's former Top 40 station. They came up with the idea of dipole antennas, the down and dirty version of which was a simple TV antenna cable split in two to make a T-shape which, when held perpendicular to the station's signal, vastly improved reception. I hit the streets with this new technical wonder, and Tom and Larry hit the airwaves, offering free diagrams on how to receive our signal loud and clear.

Suddenly, all hell broke loose for us. Every store in town with any interest in the hipster subculture was playing our station exclusively and the KMPX lobby was packed continually with freaks looking for the antenna diagram.

Just as suddenly, I was selling time, too. I think the first sponsor I brought in was Don Weir's Music City, a small North Beach shop that sold instruments, amplifiers and everything else for the musician. The Family Dog's Avalon Ballroom and Bill Graham's Fillmore also jumped on board early.

More DJs could be brought on now. Bob McClay, another former Top 40 guy, took 2 pm until 6 pm, Bob Postel spun those platters in the 10 am to 2 pm spot and Bob Prescott filled out the weekday clock from 6 am to 10 am Carl Gottlieb and Howard Hesseman each took weekend shifts, I took one also (under the name of The Lone Ranger because of my past with the FBI) and the man who taught us all about the blues, Voco (Abe Kesh), filled the critical Saturday night shift.

Donahue added the "chick engineers": Dusty Street (whom I recruited from San Francisco State), Suzie Creamcheese and Katie Johnson.

Sales were smokin' so I brought on more guys to help: Jack Towle, an original Family Dog member, Chan Laughlin (whom we got released from jail with a letter guaranteeing him employment), and Whitney Harris, the first "straight" salesman.

By the end of May 1967 (minutes before the fateful Summer of Love) we were broadcasting 24 hours a day, seven days a week.

A simple concept had emerged. Not from any one of us, but from us all:

1) Identify the audience (the few hundreds or thousands of us dancing to each other's music, selling each other drugs, fucking ourselves flat, and laughing ourselves silly. Those of us that half-hoped the entire world would catch on and enjoy the fun while simultaneously hoping the word would not get out and blow our cover. Obviously, Scott McKenzie's "If You're Goin' to San Francisco, Be Sure to Wear Some Flowers in Your Hair" had not yet hit the charts.

2) Play the music to that audience that it was playing to itself but provide a broader spectrum of it than any one individual had mastered. And play it in stereo.

3) Advertise only those products and services that we were already consuming, like the Avalon and Fillmore dance halls, the Haight-Ashbury head shops, and the music equipment stores. We produced the spots ourselves so they fit the sound and came on more like a recommendation from a friend than a harangue by a used car salesman. Pimple creams and other "middle class" agency ads were not even to be considered.

The powerful tell-it-like-it-is (especially in the case of the Vietnam War) news department had not occurred to us at this early stage and would not develop until we moved over to KSAN in 1968). The news guys are especially important: Larry Lee, Dave McQueen, Wes "Scoop" Nisker ("If you don't like the news, go out and make some of your own!"), Peter Laufer, Chan (Travis T. Hipp) Laughlin. These are the guys who went at the Vietnam War head-on, no-holds-barred.

Tom Donahue's role in all of this cannot be overstated. He was Big Daddy to us all. He didn't develop this concept on his own, but as new people came at him with their own ideas he broadened his vision to incorporate them. He would wing it until he could verbalize it, then he'd sell it to back to us.

I had a half-baked notion at the time called the IOU Theory. Basically, it's that in any given money-generating entity people fall into one of three categories: Innovators, Operators, and Underwriters. The Innovators have all the ideas, but ideas is all they have. They are the artists, geniuses and inventors who have no idea of how to capitalize on their innovations. The Operators have only one idea, to make money by exploiting the Innovators. The Underwriters have no idea at all, they simply indulge themselves in the inventions of the Innovators by paying the Operators to do so.

As I watched Tom I hoped we would be able to combine the first two parts of this theory into one, to synthesize a revolutionary concept in radio while making a living at it too.

I think Larry Miller never got the credit he deserves for being the first on the air at KMPX or for taking those first few swings with the mighty sledge of free-form radio that knocked tightly formatted Top 40 rock radio on its ass, for a few years anyway.

Larry really did create the entire prototype of what came to be known as underground radio on his midnight to 6 am shift. He found KMPX before any of us, talked the management (Leon Crosby, owner, and Ron Hunt, general manager) into letting him have a shift which he would pay for by selling ads to local businesses frequented by counterculture types. He played the "other," longer and hipper cuts off albums instead of only the short lead singles, he mixed styles of music, and he didn't shout at his audience. The basics! Right there.

Unfortunately, Larry had a few strikes against him that prevented him from being considered a leader like Donahue or an innovator like Abe (Voco) Kesh. Attitude and taste: his were both terrible.

Larry was pissed off from the git-go when Tom Donahue came on board and assumed a position of leadership. I think Larry felt that Big Daddy was a reject from Top 40 (I believe Tom had been ushered out of KYA for some payola scandal) and that Tom knew little about free-form programming as Larry envisioned it. Larry, alone all night long on his shift, let this or something eat away at him. Some say he was a juicer rather than a pot smoker like the rest of us. All I know is that he was one grumpy motherfucker when he came into work and even worse when he left in the morning.

Larry's advertising was pretty much limited to places he frequented, like Larry Blake's in Berkeley (where he ate and drank before coming in to work), so he wasn't really generating much income for the station.

Perhaps his worst sin in that heady era was that he was not in tune with the drug culture, the bulk of our audience. He could put a few interesting music segues together, but more often than not he would lull the audience into a mellow mood with an Indian raja rather than whip it upside the head with a fucking Spike Jones barn burner. He'd do this at four in the morning when many listeners were coming down from acid trips. He was out of sync with his listeners or listening to only a few with very bizarre and grating palettes. But, indeed, he was there first and should not be overlooked by history.

Tom Donahue! Where to begin?

He was older than the rest of us by at least a decade (most of us were in our mid-twenties) and eons ahead in experience. If I'm correct, Tom had been with US Army Intelligence in the Philippines during the early to mid-Fifties. Once out, he moved to Philadelphia and got into Top 40 radio and rock 'n' roll with the Alan Freeds and Dick Clarks of the time.

I saw photos of Tom in those days: standing before a microphone was a tall, thin-as-a-rail, dark-haired man with an Adam's apple the size of Alcatraz. Half the man I met in 1967 who by then had grown into his voice: way over 300 pounds and still blooming, a man of insatiable appetites for fine food, dangerous drugs and mind-bending music.

And cool? The man had enough for everyone in town!

I remember getting my knickers in a knot one day a few months after we had gone to 24-hour-a-day programming. Revenue was no longer coming in from foreign language and religious programs, so the entire burden of the station's financial survival was on my shoulders. Suddenly Ron Hunt, the general manager, slapped the transmitter electricity bill onto my desk. It was a whopper: $3,000. We had 72 hours to pay it or we would be executed. Our signal would go off the air, certain death to our newborn underground radio baby.

I dashed out of the building and spent the next two days pleading with our advertisers for advances on the money they owed us. We had more than enough account receivables by now, but I met with serious disappointment across the board. Bill Graham was maniacally building his empire and way too tight to come up with a nickel before it was due and Chet Helms was way too disorganized to know if he even had any money to spare; all the retail stores (head shops, clothing, records and musical instrument stores) were doing so well because of our advertising that they had reinvested all their cash in more inventory.

KMPX was instantly in deep, deep trouble.

Just hours before the deadline on the final day, I damn near broke down. I walked into Tom's office and told him the full story as I saw it. The station was fucked and it was my fault! I had let him down, and all the other staff. Tom asked enough questions to ascertain I had indeed covered all the bases. Then he sat in silence, contemplating his options. He began to roll a joint as he watched me wind myself tighter and tighter.

In near tears I finally said, "I'm sorry, Tom. I've handled lots of problems around here but this one is beyond me. I've tried everything I can think but I'm out of strokes, Tom. I'm sorry."

Tom leaned across his desk, handed the joint to me, and whispered with tones from the bottom of a baritone sax.

"Milan," he said, "don't worry. I'll take care of everything."

I've hardly ever felt such relief. Big Daddy was the right handle for this cat. He would indeed keep us on the air somehow. We were safe in his care.

I strolled back to my office, lit the joint, and kicked back to enjoy the pleasant ride. At last, I was off the hook. I was out of the crosshairs. I was out from under the giant thumb. I was loaded and loving it!

I was loving all the dope dealers in town who brought fists full of this fine weed to our station and gave it to us in appreciation of all the good music we were broadcasting.

Then it hit me! Dope dealers! They couldn't advertise on the air but they sure as hell could help when we were in a jam. I phoned mine, a close friend I had grown up with. I explained the situation: Three grand within the hour or we'd go off the air.

"No problem," he said. He'd go out back and dig it up. "Why didn't you ask sooner?"

And indeed he had.

All of us would learn plenty from Tom about cool.

Leon Crosby, the owner of KMPX, was anything but cool. He was a nervous, mousy little character with a pencil-thin moustache who wore a cheap rug and dyed his protruding tufts to match. We seldom saw Leon.

Tom Donahue

He seemed terrified of us longhairs. We had taken over his hardware and he dealt with us through Ron Hunt, his general manager.

Ron was middle-class, as we used to say back then, remarkably indistinguishable from tens of millions of other mid-Westerners. He wasn't a bad guy; he just didn't have a clue about what was whirling all about him either. Numbers made plain sense to him, though. He could see the money beginning to pour in and might even have had an idea of the potential of this new formatless format. He knew he had had nothing to do with this success, so he slipped off into the wings and became, in effect, the bookkeeper.

Ron and Leon would come back center stage about a year after we started this new programming. Technically, Leon owned the license and Ron managed it for him; but those of us who had created the sound reasoned we owned it. That led to the huge clash between "them" and "us." In the summer of 1968 it culminated in a staff strike that sent all of us out onto the streets and later on to KSAN.

Raechel Donahue was not really a player at KMPX. She was a go-go dancer when Tom talked her offstage a few years before to help him with Autumn Records, his one-hit ("The Swim" by Bobby Freeman) record company. (Go-go dancer is not a put-down. Though I was dating Janis Joplin at the time, if that's what you'd call dating, I was technically still married to a "foxy" – another term of the time – go-go dancer myself.) Raechel would begin to stretch her lovely wings on the airwaves later at KSAN and, in the late seventies and eighties, became a powerhouse on the radio in LA. But in 1967 the most we heard on the air from Rae was the sound of seeds rolling around in a shoebox lid as she cleaned weed and rolled joints for Tom.

All of us on the air (I was pulling only one shift per week, plus the odd fill-in for someone sick or too gooned to make it in) were influencing each other, as well as the audience. But the single strongest influence was Abe (Voco) Kesh, an Armenian hipster from Chicago with a vast knowledge of the blues and a passion to play nothing but. He took the strategic Saturday night from 6 pm until midnight spot and was maybe single-handedly responsible for turning the audience on to musicians like BB King, Howlin' Wolf, John Lee Hooker, and the white blues guys like Paul Butterfield, Charlie Musslewhite, and John Mayall. Later on, at KSAN, he was the first in the nation to air the Edwin Hawkins Singers ("Oh, Happy Day") and he would go on to become a record producer for Mercury-Phillips (and to get me the same job with them).

Sometime after the station's sound was set, Tom hired Edward Bear (aka Stephen Hirsh). If my memory serves, and the closer to geezerdom I get, the more senior moments, the more sails on Golden Pond I experience, Bear replaced Larry Miller and the all-night shift got way more mellow.

In many ways Bear was the perfect guy to have on your radio from midnight to dawn during the Summer of Love. He broadcast none of the negativity of Larry Miller, had an excellent ear for the segue, and tirelessly promoted peace and love. His girlfriend, Goldie, was the ultimate flower child.

KMPX was the Pied Piper of the Summer of Love in San Francisco. When people were not playing music of their own or listening to it live at the ballrooms or concerts, they were hearing it from us. Once the T-antennas got around, the sound was everywhere. One could walk down the street in the Haight-Ashbury or North Beach or Polk Gulch or Castro Street and pop in and out of shops or pass by groups of people sitting in parks with portable radios and hear only KMPX. It was possible to dash all around town for an entire day and never be out of earshot of the signal. That applied to Berkeley and southern Marin County, too.

The audience impacted the air staff as well. The phone rang constantly in the DJ/engineer's booth and more often than not audience members would call in to thank us for playing the exact tune that they had wanted. It was almost spooky at first. The DJs seemed to be tapping into some collective consciousness and the audience was making the real programming decisions. After a while this connection became so commonplace that none of us on the air even mentioned it. We took it for granted that we were not always the ones making the choice of which tune to segue into next. It sounds hippie-ish, I know, but not one among us would deny that this happened to some degree.

It was very common for bands to drop by the station to promote an album or appearance and end up in the booth and on the air with Donahue, Bob McClay, and Edward Bear. John Fogerty, Paul Kantner (Airplane /Starship), and Bob Weir (Grateful Dead) were there often.

We tried to make on-air ads sound like personal endorsements. In fact our hope was that they would be. Each time we got a new account, I asked the DJ whose show would air the ad to visit the advertiser, to see if there was something in the shop that tripped their imagination, something they could yammer enthusiastically about for 60 seconds. Often I provided fact sheets the DJs could use to remind them of the store and its merchandise; for obvious reasons we avoided written copy. Reading copy verbatim sounded just like reading copy verbatim and that was way out of sync with what we were trying to do on the air.

It was the Sixties and in the course of a morning's round of business appointments a person could get loaded by Chet Helms at the Avalon, laid by Peggy Caserta at Mnasidikaís, or tongue-lashed by Bill Graham at the Fillmore.

I always made my weekly call to Graham's office the first call of the day. I knew he would be sitting there at seven or eight in the morning, wearing two watches (one for local time, one for NY) yelling into his phone. I could picture some New York agent or band manager on the other end of the line, holding the receiver at arm's length and wincing as Graham screamed his threat not to book his band(s) into the Fillmore ever again if the agent allowed any of the horses in his stable to work for the Avalon, the Carousel, or "any fucking body else who tries to sell music in this town!"

For a Jew who survived Hitler's concentration camps, Bill Grajonka was quite the Nazi himself. If you ask me, and I know you didn't, Bill Graham was the single strongest negative influence on the San Francisco scene in the Sixties. He raised the level of competition and lowered the standards of fair play to such a degree that one had to throw ethics out the window and stoop to his level just to stay in the game.

The "benefit concerts" Graham produced were mere crumbs compared to the near obscene profits he amassed. He still scares people from the grave through Bill Graham Productions. Say anything bad about Bill, Bucko, and you ain't invited back.

As the Summer of Love dawned, those of us who had promoted recreational drug use had to wake up to one of its uglier realities: bad acid and massive consumption of it. San Francisco was suddenly the Mecca for counterculture pilgrims. They were pouring into town by the bus-plane-train-car load, and bad bathtub acid was raining down on us all.

What later became a valuable organized community drug information service at KSAN under the guidance of people like Dr. Hipp (Gene Schoenfeld) started at KMPX. Often a listener would appear in the KMPX lobby with some pills in a baggie and a message not to take them. A DJ like Bob McClay would invite the listener into the booth, have him describe the pill on the air and describe its effects. It was the best we could do.

At this point, the underground sound was a success on all levels. We're broadcasting round the clock every day of the week. We're the most popular sound in town among the emerging subculture. To everyone's surprise we're even appearing strong in the Arbitron ratings. Ad space is almost entirely sold out and clients accept our raise in rates without a whimper. Only problem now is that the air staff and engineers are getting less than peanuts for their good work.

They argue rightly that they are the sound. Since there is no playlist, each air staffer makes his own decision as to what to play when and between what and what else. This takes homework to do well. Every record company in the world is showering us with promo copies of their entire catalogue. When the DJs are not playing records on the air, they are listening to the new albums at home and it takes all day every day to keep up.

We raise the ad rates a tad more, but Leon Crosby through Ron Hunt argues that there's still not enough spare money to give the DJs and engineers their due. We all can add and it's obvious to us all that Crosby is keeping the lion's share. "Back debt," he argues, which may be true, but we joke that he's also supporting his sidesqueeze's failing beauty parlor on our nickel.

Donahue and I agree it's time to approach the "establishment" advertising agencies. We naively assume that they will listen to our pitch: that we can sell their products, like Pepsi, to our audience better than they can with their Top 40 jingles and that they should give us tons of money to produce spots for their products that will be consistent with our sound.

I book several appointments at agencies, and Tom and I hit them together. The two of us have to laugh about our impact on the agency personnel. He is six feet two inches and over 350 pounds by now, with shoulder length black hair, a massive black beard, and is dressed in all black: black sport coat over black pants and black turtleneck. I am the same height, thin as a rail, literally weighing in less than half of him, sporting dark hair that hangs straight to my waist and fitted into a mod suit with tie. We walk through these agency outer offices and typing pools to the accompaniment of stifled gasps, chins dropping onto desks, and the whispered questions like, "Who would have booked an appointment with those two muggers from outer space?"

One courageous ad account exec, Dawn Tagnoli, who handles Pepsi in the Bay Area, actually seems receptive to the idea of us selling Pepsi to our audience in our own way. However, accepting Establishment advertisers, specifically Pepsi, became an issue for argument among the KMPX staff. Half the crew was dead set against any and all Establishment products. The other half pointed to the empty Pepsi and Coke cans lying all around the station and reasoned that it would be hypocritical not to accept their advertising money. I hoped a middle ground could be found. If Dawn Tagnoli could get Pepsi's permission for us to create an ad for them that was in sync with our sound, everybody would come out ahead.

But it was not to be. Dawn tried, or at least she told me she did. The woman went all the way to top levels of Pepsi's corporate headquarters before she was told no.

This was one of the issues that led to the strike in May of 1968.

Not too many months before the strike, Donahue caught the interest of Lew Avery, a gentle grandfatherly type who had been in radio almost since Marconi. Tom knew him from KYA. Tom also knew that Lew knew a good thing when he saw its ratings raging, so he got Lew to head a group of investors who agreed to fund our expansion into the Los Angeles market.

Tom and Lew found KPPC, another station losing money running religious and foreign programming. The initials stood for Pasadena Presbyterian Church. The station resided in its basement. I believe our first broadcasts from there were in March of 1968.

For a brief period before the strike Tom and I were flying back and forth to Burbank airport almost daily to work both on and off the air on this new station. Before too long Tom brought a friend, B. Mitchell Reed, another disgruntled veteran of Top 40, to KPPC to anchor evening music until midnight.

We were thinking now of going national.

Once the sound of underground radio was set at KMPX and we became successful, the rift grew between Leon Crosby/Ron Hunt and the staff that had created this free-form success.

The sound was personality-driven. It wasn't the music alone that made underground radio what is was. It was also the people who put the music together for the audience, people who offered their vast knowledge of that music with such honest enthusiasm, people who loved the sound we were creating, people who were part of the community listening to that music.

Leon Crosby didn't give a rat's ass about the sound. The music and the people who played it ran a distant last to the bucks they generated. Broadcasting hippos farting underwater would have worked for him if it brought in the cash.

When issues like the Pepsi jingle surfaced and Leon discovered that we were even remotely considering not accepting the money to air the ad, it pushed him over the edge. This man who was nowhere to be seen during the station's perpetual financial crisis, who had zero to do with creating its sound or success, suddenly appeared on the set and started to exert control. Reaction among staffers, yours truly included, was "Who the fuck is this guy and where does he tend bar?"

The chasm widened between Leon/Ron and the staff. The on-air and off-air staffs wanted a bigger piece of the cash flowing in and those of us on the sales staff (who were making good money on commissions alone) wanted unfettered creative control of advertising policy.

Increasingly nasty meetings took place between Ron Hunt, Tom Donahue and me.

One of the minor issues was the length of my hair. Leon suggested through Ron that I cut my hair so I would be more presentable to advertising agencies. That was the straw that broke this particular camel's back. I could see Leon would never go back into his hole, so I joined the conspiracy to strike.

And strike we did.

There must be an air-check somewhere of the last words we spoke on the air just before we went out into the street to meet the crowd of listeners that had come to support us.

The strike lasted most of the summer of 1968. At first we seemed to have one hundred percent community support. Ron Hunt put a scab on-air crew together, but all the advertisers cancelled their spots. Bands who would have been coming in for on-air interviews came instead to play benefits for us strikers. Chet Helms, Ron Rackow, and Bill Graham at the Avalon, Carousel and Fillmore/Winterland ballrooms, respectively, allowed us stage time between sets to explain our case to their audiences.

We seemed to have everything going for us. Everything but a sound. Our spirit, the sound without a signal, was eventually worn down by attrition. One of the strikers broke with the on-the-street staff and went back into KMPX. The "benefit concerts" were dwindling and so was the strike fund that kept us alive. Perhaps worst of all, a stone cold stalemate existed between Crosby and his erstwhile staff. Crosby was glad to be rid of us troublemakers and we troublemakers could not in our worst nightmares imagine going back to work for him.

In August I was approached by Stefan Ponek, a DJ at KSFR, Metromedia's classical music station in San Francisco, and its sales manager. As one of the strike leaders, virtually second-in-command after Donahue (that is, if there had been a chain of command) and, perhaps more important to Metromedia's moguls, the guy holding the keys to a vault packed with advertisers eager to get back on the air, I was asked if I thought the striking KMPX staff would come over to Metromedia.

On first hearing, the idea sounded like a lifesaver.

But there was fine print.

Worse, there was a deal breaker: Tom Donahue was not invited. I told Stefan that I would communicate their proposal to the striking staff, but that I was positive that no one would consider going anywhere without Tom. It was all of us or none. Take it or leave it!

The objection to Tom was dropped, and he joined the negotiations with Metromedia. The striking KMPX and KPPC staffs voted overwhelmingly to move out of the striking business and back into broadcasting. In San Francisco we went to work for what became KSAN; in LA the staff went over to KMEL.

Not all of us walked into the new station crying tears of joy. I, for one, felt it was the beginning of the end of free-form, personality-driven, playlist-free, honesty-in-advertising radio. How could one use "underground" and "Metromedia Incorporated" in the same sentence?

I went through the motions to insure a smooth transition from the street back to the air for our staff and advertisers but my heart was elsewhere. (At the moment, it was actually with Mimi Farina whom I married in September of that year.)

Abe Kesh, Voco, arranged the job for me at Mercury-Phillips. He had produced a hit, "Summertime Blues," with Blue Cheer and he asked me to produce their second album. I had a new career and, though I still did part-time work on the air at KSAN, my interest in radio had exited stage left.

But let me be clear here. Wonderfully creative, inventive, and entertaining times were had at KSAN and the offspring it spawned, especially in their news and talk time. In fact most of what people remember as underground radio in San Francisco happened at KSAN. KMPX had lasted only a year but KSAN carried on for I-dunno-how-long!

In the fall of 1972, after a year in Nepal, two things were very clear to me: one, I wanted to spend the rest of my existence in the Himalayas, and two, I didn't have the money to do so. With tail tucked between my legs, I flew back to SF and asked Donahue for work. We cooked up an idea and pitched it to Bill Graham. He agreed.

The end result was a 72-hour marathon broadcast I remember only by the name The Fillmore Special. Bill Graham brought scores of live Fillmore recordings, I brought hours of edited interviews I'd done with many band members, and we met on the air at KSAN. Bill then sat with each DJ on his shift as I fed the DJ the musician interviews to match the live recordings. (Except for a few winks on the floor, Graham stayed awake for all three days and nights.)

Back in Nepal several months later, I heard Thom O'Hair had edited the show and it won the Armstrong Award, a prestigious award for FM radio broadcasting.

Midway through interviewing all these musicians, I realized that everyone was praising Graham like some kind of god. The overall statement of the interviews was rapidly deteriorating into sentimental adulation and Graham worship. I started asking each interviewee for something other than ass-kissing about Graham, but it continued unabated.

When I asked Bobby Weir for some balance to this litany of praise, all he would say was, "Well, Bill's a real competitor. When he plays baseball he'll push you out of the way if you're standing between him and the base."

That wasn't exactly what I was looking for, so I kept digging. I realized every damn musician in town depended on Bill for their livelihood, but I was stunned at how afraid of him they actually were.

Finally I cornered Honest Nicky the Greek. Gravenites told the story on tape of one of Graham's rages. Bill, he said, had told Janis and her band not to smoke weed backstage anymore. Janis was Janis, of course, and ignored him. When she returned to the green room after her set, Graham was already hiding in the armoire waiting for the smell of smoke. Eventually it reached him. He burst from the armoire, grabbed Janis by the neck, escorted her to the entrance, no doubt shouting all the way, and threw her down the stairs!

Cut to the KSAN booth during the Fillmore show: I was doing an air shift myself and aired the interview with Gravenites telling the Janis story as Bill Graham sat next to me. I've seen my share of Graham tirades, but the mike was open, we were live on the air, and Graham could only do a slow burn. I do remember him going extremely red. Janis had been dead only two years and the loss was still fresh and painful to many.

Cut to a few years later, I'm back in SF for a brief visit and I run into Gravenites.

"How's it going?" I ask him.

"Terrible!" he replies. "Graham never hired me again after that interview I did for you!" And, as far as I know, to this day Bill Graham Productions still hasn't.

No joy remained in radio for me after that. We had lost, I thought, our chance to do anything significant. I was wrong when it came to the news department at KSAN, but that wasn't my scene. I was always appreciative of what did happen in the news department, but still I thought if we'd had our own radio station even that could have been better. I wasn't interested in sales anymore because Metromedia began to bring in its own corporate sales people. I wasn't in charge in sales, as I had been at KMPX. I started looking for other ways to make money.

7

SCREAMIN' JAY HAWKINS

Vaco got me hooked up with Mercury-Phillips. They figured because I was a DJ, because I was on the air, that I could get my fellow DJs to play their records. They gave the assignment of producing Blue Cheer's second album, sort of under the wing of Vaco.

Neither of us really knew what we were doing. We were not musicians. We'd never produced records before. We basically booked the sessions and made sure that everybody got paid for them and then let the engineer do the real producing.

The Blue Cheer album, their second album after *Summertime Blues*, was a nightmare for me because it wasn't about the music, it was about the money and the little fifteen minutes of fame that they had. Most of what I did was keep them out of jail for bringing home hookers and bringing hookers to the hotel, and that was not fun. We got through it, we made the album okay, and it – rightfully – died, and that was that.

I did a second album that I did enjoy with Lynn Hughes and Michael Ferguson called *Tongue and Groove*. They were friends and I did have some input on those sessions and I liked the album. That was fun.

The third album I did was with a group called Linn County and it was okay, but not that great.

The album I really enjoyed, the one that just knocked me out, was the Screaming Jay Hawkins album with "Feast of the Mau-mau" and "Constipation Blues." I enjoyed that so much because Jay was out there from the minute I met him. The minute I met him I knew this was going be a hoot.

I tracked Jay down to a club. He was the emcee at a strip joint in Honolulu called Forbidden City, a strip joint for the military.

Jay would be standing up on stage between the strippers and the drunk sailors would be shouting, "Hey, cocksucker, get off the stage. Bring on the tits."

Jay would say, "You call me a cocksucker man, you're the one with the scratches behind your ears."

Jay had been heckled and hassled all those years and he just took nothing off of nobody. He was a former Golden Gloves boxing champion.

I proposed the album to Mercury and they liked the idea because Jay was the founding father of shock rock. Arthur Brown and Doctor John and Alice Cooper, they were beginning to come on at that time. They all found the origin for their shock rock back in Screaming Jay Hawkins.

He came on stage in a coffin, with a mirror in the lid, lying in the coffin there with him was a skull on a stick, named Henry, with luminous bright red eyes. Henry would smoke a cigarette. That was just for openers. That was before his act even started.

Jay was a very bizarre dude. He told me wonderful stories of his partner "Shoutin' Pat." In the late Fifties, they did an album, *Screamin' Jay and Shoutin' Pat in Hong Kong*. Pat swung both ways which, in the beginning, Jay loved because when she brought her girls home he "got to fuck 'em bof." But Pat soon started "claimin' exclusivity on that pussy." One night, Jay went for her girl and "she shot me three times. When I fell down she tried to cut me in half with a knife. I got up and chased that bitch for three and a half blocks before I passed out."

Jay had not been back to the mainland since the mob ran him off for the absolutely unacceptable act of attempting to collect a portion of the royalties due him for "I Put a Spell on You." I brought him back for the recording session, and housed him on the top floor of the Chateau Marmont in a suite between Albert Grossman and Art Garfunkle (or some other icon of peace and love). When I came to pick him up I found him sleeping on the couch by the front door.

I asked him why he would sleep on the couch when he had such a huge bed in the bedroom. Tiptoeing, with finger to his lips, he led me over to the window where he had driven a nail with his shoe into the stucco wall and tied the two ends of a dynamite detonating cap to the nail and to the window handle "in case they find out I'm back and try to get me this way."

The fact that the window was five stories above the ground and there was no exterior fire escape within sight meant nothing to him.

"They don't forget," he told me.

After the album was done we wanted to send him out on tour, so I asked him what he needed in the way of props.

He said, "A fold-up African cookin' pot, some dry ice, a mannequin, a bottle of ketchup, a machete, and I'll do all the rest."

I only did those four albums. And a single, a lovely little single by Mitch Greenhill, called "There Ain't No Instant Replay in the Football Game of Life," which I think says it all.

8

ACROSS THE USA WITH THE MEDICINE BALL CARAVAN

This record career was going nowhere and somebody, not me or Donahue, came up with the idea of taking Warner Brothers music acts on the road and putting on more or less impromptu concerts across America with Warner Brothers acts, like BB King and Jefferson Airplane and Pink Floyd. The idea was to go from spot to spot, from venue to venue, by caravan, a hundred and sixty of us in thirty vehicles. On the road we would make a documentary out of this caravan, filming the performances of these artists. It sounded like a good thing.

The film crew however, had come from France, with France's foremost documentarian, François Reichenbach. They came not with the idea of doing as professional a job as possible but instead seeing it as an opportunity to consume as much psychedelic as possible. It turned into a drug fest and they missed the best events. They never even filmed the best of what went down. A terrible movie came out about it.

When we got to Paris, the editors of the film realized that there was no connection between the film and the sound. One of the French film crew guys would be standing there with a number seven on his slate and he would go mark five. They were trying to edit it together and couldn't. In Paris they hired a couple of us to help them figure out whose voices were whose. They finally managed to get the sound synched to the picture, but they missed so much of the film. Out of hundreds of hours of film probably fifty hours were focusing in and out of a Coca-Cola cup on the grass next to a cigarette butt, you know, where the camera operator had seen God.

The worst of that mess was when we had Pink Floyd at Canterbury, England. We had seven cameras working. "A" camera, the number one camera, was on the boom doing all of these very avant-garde swoops in and out of the band during this long three-hour Pink Floyd performance.

They never put film in the camera.

The camera operators were convinced that what they were seeing was being electronically transferred back into the van or something, I don't know. But there was no fucking film in the camera.

From Paris, in a September 1970 letter to Carl Gottlieb, Milan summed up the trip with irritation:

Mainly, I remember working my ass off. Donahue spent most of his time hollering at the assholes at Warner Brothers from a telephone in a motel room. Chan spent all off his time fucking around with the shower tepee and sneaking into the refrigerator truck. Jack Towle spent most of his time screaming, "The candy-ass sons of bitches!" It seems to me I did nothing but answer questions about money, laundry, diapers, routes, concerts, busts, campsites and teepee set-ups. It seems I did it all, but I know everybody was up against the same wall – too fast, too hard, too soon!

Before we departed SF we decided to dose the film crew, which we did too well. François said after about ten days out, "The world had lost fifteen Frenchmen and gained fifteen freaks," which was really fine at the time but resulted in near-disaster in the editing room.

But as he told the story again thirty-one years later in Puerto Vallarta, the memories made Milan smile.

Tom Donahue scribbled across the front vehicle, "We have come for your daughters." After the first concert that we put on in Boulder, Colorado, word rolled ahead of us that the hippies, the druggies were on the way. When we reached the border of Nebraska every guy with a uniform was there to meet us at the border. Not only all the Highway Patrol and the policemen and the National Guard uniforms, but there were guys in World War II uniforms. There were guys in Postal outfits. There were guys in Cub Scout uniforms. They all showed up to tell us that we were not going take any of their daughters.

They made us circle our wagons into a field and wait until morning and then they were going to escort us all the way across the state so that we didn't ever light foot in Nebraska. The odd thing was the field they put us into was full of turkey weed, weed that had been cultivated since World War I as hemp fields. We looked up and found ourselves surrounded by police and army walking in this seven- and eight-foot tall marijuana plant field. Unfortunately, though we tried to dry it and smoke it and get high, there wasn't a high in the whole field. It was all turkey weed.

We rolled across the States and we did our concerts. When we got to New York the idea was to take the whole crew to Europe with us. Warner Brothers was kind enough to put me and my Harley on the same airplane. As wagon master, I rode a Harley all through the film.

I arrived in England, went to the back of the plane, had the baggage handlers roll my Harley out of the baggage compartment and I rode my Harley through immigration and customs in England. Not bad for the first time that a kid from East Oakland has been out of the States, right?

I'm thinking this is pretty good here. I had a bunch of money in my pocket, from the first leg of the film, and my Harley in Europe. Everywhere I went I instantly attracted followers. I would just go to the corner store to get some milk and all of a sudden there were seventeen guys on mopeds behind me. It was very, very weird.

I spent not too long there in London and then went to Paris to work on helping them sync the sound. In October of 1970 Janis Joplin suddenly died. That threw me for a loop like I've never been thrown before. She was not only the first contemporary to die, but also the woman that I loved. I just didn't know what to do with myself. I felt her reappear, I just went out and rode through the night, through the Paris streets and I felt her reappear on the back of the bike and give me a squeeze like she used to as we were riding around, a goodbye squeeze.

9

ON TO MOROCCO

It was cold, it was dank, it was wet Paris in late October and I just wanted to get out of there. I headed south on my own to Morocco. After three days of being refused at the border I was granted permission to enter Morocco in my California Hell's Angels outfit on my Harley chopper.

On the boat somebody recommended that if I wanted some kif, some Moroccan hash, that I should go to the Café Royale and ask for Akmed.

I went, I asked, and sure enough Akmed said, "Yeah, how much do you want?"

I bought about an ounce of kif and he gave me a pipe and gave me some matches and I was set. I just sat there drinking my mint tea and shaving off my kif and smoking and about the time that I got good and high the army arrived and shut the door on the place.

Their leader said, "Everybody up against the wall."

There were about fifteen, eighteen of us off of the same ferryboat who'd all gotten the same advice, probably from the same guy, and like chumps we were all lined up against the wall and we all had our balls of hash that we just bought off of Akmed, who probably worked for the army, and what you do when you're caught up against the wall and you got drugs on you, you just drop them, right?

I dropped my stash and I kicked it, a little golf ball-sized stash, away from myself. I noticed people were all dropping their stashes and kicking them away from themselves. It was a soccer game of hashish golf balls, people were kicking hash all over the fucking room.

Eventually a bunch of it ended up at my feet just the lieutenant in charge of the operation, said to me, "You in the leathers, come here."

I thought, "Oh, fuck man. He's going to pin the whole thing on me."

I walk over to him and he said, "You can leave."

I said, "Me?"

He said, "Yeah."

I went outside and there were two women waiting, French women that I had been living with in Paris. Coincidentally they had arrived a couple days before me and were walking down the street when they looked in and saw the commotion at the Royale, including a tall guy up against the wall involved in this soccer game of hashish balls. They called the lieutenant outside and promised him sexual favors if he would let the tall one in the leathers go.

They asked me, "Do you want to come up to our hotel room?"

I said, "Absolutely. I want to do anything you want to do."

We went up to their hotel room and they said, "Look, now that you're out, we know you have a little money left from the movie, how about you give us your money and in three days our friend Rasheed will buy hash and triple your money. Three times as much money in three days."

Having just come out of the frying pan, I wasn't too interested in jumping into the fire.

I said, "Yes, okay. I'll be right back up. The money's in my handlebars."

I went downstairs and kicked the Harley over and just kept going south until I stuck the axle in the sand way down south below Agadir and arrived in a village where the road ran out. There was no more road going south in Morocco. That's where I lived for about six months with Moroccan fishermen. Licking my wounds over the Janis loss.

During this period Milan sent a barrage of letters home, often to his friend Carl Gottlieb, such as this fragment detailing his experiences getting a visa extension from the Minister of Tourism during a party that started with a police raid:

Frydman starts groping for Barbara with greasy hands, Eddie is starting to get itchy because he left his outfit at home and he's now in the second month of this monkey, and I hit on the Minister for an extension of my visa because, if we are going to do a movie in Mirleft, I'll need special clearance with the police. The Minister has some flunky call the commander of all the police, and all the rest of the Anglos chime in with requests for extensions – granted – all of us. Three seconds later the Police Commander comes in walking on his knees thinking he's fucked up somehow. The Commander hears the request of the Minister's flunky for our extension and says weakly that we'll have to cut our hair to get an extension. The Minister flashes him a look that put pee-pee down his leg and he tries to explain that he was only making a very poor little joke – wrecked his whole career, I'm sure.

Milan sent a request letter home for a care package of motorcycle parts for his 1965 FLH Harley-Davidson Electra Glide:

With these parts I can stay on the road forever and send interesting letters home and find more pirate ships and cause some scenes. Also, imagine trying to find a voltage regulator in Senegal or Kenya!

By the time Milan wrote this to his father from Morocco, he was sure of his future.

Dad,

Prepare yourself in the beginning. I need to borrow $150 from you. But it won't be long before I can pay it back. It looks like Carl Gottlieb got work for me in another film. So I'll have lots of money again soon.

The reason my plans got screwed up is because Jack Towle has not sold my bus as of yet. This loan is a precaution, of course. From the tone of Carl's letter, they'll be sending for me soon. But, just in case, I think I should ask for the loan. If the film falls through, I plan to go to Paris, sell the Harley, repay you for the loan and fly to India. Sound safe enough?

I hope so, because we both know I can't count on any of my friends to loan me the bread. Everyone I know is like me: sometimes in the money, sometimes out.

I don't know exactly how to explain myself to you these days. But I feel it necessary, somehow, to try. I have more or less decided to make my living in the arts. By this I mean movies and writing. People seem to want me in their movies. I don't really know why, maybe it is the way I look or because of my organizational abilities or something different about me. So I may end up rich and famous. Most likely I'll make a few bucks now and then.

Some of the things I've written lately have led me (and some other people) to believe I have writing abilities.

In order to further these ends, to develop and enrich myself, to become more aware and educated, I want to travel.

I have to travel, to see, sit with, drink tea with, eat, sleep, and shit with all the people of the world: the old fishermen, the farmers, the camel herders, the pygmies, the presidents, the businessmen, the women, etc., etc. You name it, I want to see it. I know I'll have to go to the offices, the oceans, the deserts, the jungles, the cafés and the mountains of the world to do it. But I've got to try.

As you know, I've never been one that liked the nine to five, day after day, or the same job too long. I've got moving in my bones, and I've got to obey it or be unhappy the rest of my life.

I've never really been great in school, even though I got great grades in the early days. But I did capture the most important message you ever gave me and that was to "learn to learn." I know how to learn very rapidly. I've learned radio, movies, languages, and now Moroccan dancing, cooking and a thousand other things. That's all I ask of life: to give me something new to learn every day.

Eventually, if I keep my eyes open, I will see something no one has ever seen. Then I can give it to the world and hope to be compensated for it. I may die a pauper, but I'll go out with a smile for having lived the life I loved.

I hope all this makes sense to you because I've just told my innermost secrets – from my heart as well as my brain.

All things are well here in Mirleft. There is sun every day. I eat great food. I exercise daily and have put on about ten pounds which is good for me. Twice a week I play soccer with the men in town. Damalek, the school teacher, bought a pair of soccer shoes for me which cost him about a week's wages. Then he refused to accept my money. I guess he's pretty happy about receiving Janelle's letter with word of all the educational materials she has sent. "I guess," hell. I know for sure. Thank you for all your help in making that happen.

Oh, back to the money for a moment. If you send money orders, please send them in $50 denominations. This way I will cash only one in Morocco. The reason I ask this is because Moroccan money isn't worth a damn outside of this country. So I'd hate to be stuck with $150 worth of useless dirhams.

Also, just as a safety measure, please phone Jack and ask him if the bus is sold before you buy the money orders. If he has sold the bus and sent me the money then I won't need the loan from you, okay?

That's it for now, back to the beach. I could dig to receive a few lines from you if you feel like it, and thanks again, Pop.

Love,
Milan

Jack sold the bus. Milan was able to cancel the loan request. This, from another letter out of Morocco:

I'm really itchy to split for places further on, further out. I've done the town of Mirleft and had it with the country of Morocco. I've danced all night with fifty Moroccans, all of us dressed in white or in sheep suits, fished during the morning, afternoon, evening and all night long, lingered between the tides, between centuries, learned to cook all the Moroccan food and drinks, walked dazedly over every inch of this small section, met and befriended everybody in town and roots are starting to sprout from my boots.

It will probably take me only three weeks to get to Dakar once I depart. It's only 1,424 miles from Dakar to Timbuktu. Timbuktu would be good for my legend and when I split from there I can barge it all the way down the Niger River to Lagos.

In the pile of letters Milan asked me to prowl through, I found this intriguing fragment from the Morocco days, addressed to Janelle.

I spent a month here alone. Then, on February 1st, a beautiful girl drove into town in her VW bus. In her bus she…

… and the next page is missing.
Another fragment from a letter to Janelle:

The only piece of advice I can give you is that in the end each of us is alone. Like all heavy things in life, it's made up of joy and sorrow. The joy of catching that rare glimpse of your real self and standing proud in its light, the sadness of so many of the changes each of us must go through on that path to ourself. Finally, though, we have only ourselves, momentary flashes of love or brotherhood for other people are only of that moment. The embarrassment, intimidation, the hassles imposed on each of us are only the result of other people's attempts to define themselves and really have very little to do with you or me.

I know so little about myself that I'm sure everybody else knows absolutely nothing about me. Our only companion on this lonely venture is the moment – each should be lived to its fullest – lived by me in my way, you in yours – whatever those ways may be. There is no judgment, there is no blame.

All of this is bullshit, of course. Again, it's only my attempt to define me and should mean very little to the real you. My old fishing buddy, Fakir Mohammed, said to me the other day, "Milan, no pensé beaucoup. Dejarlo para Alluh – El hacerlo mejor." Which means something like, "Milan, don't think so much. Leave it to God – He does a better job."

Right on, Old Man. Let's have a lot less thinking and a lot more living.

After some six months Milan was heading home to California.

I was busted out of Morocco by Carl Gottlieb. David Crosby had written a movie that Carl was going to direct and they wanted me to star in it opposite Joni Mitchell. It was a science fiction story that David had written, about going forward to the past when times were good. They flew me and the Harley back to Los Angeles. After about ten days the picture was cancelled. After having been in Morocco with an idea to be the first guy to get a Harley across Africa, suddenly I was back in LA. I was just another schlub stuck on the streets with an empty gas tank.

I went around and borrowed a hundred dollars from everybody I knew and said, "I hope you'll see it again, but I can't guarantee it," and I rode the Harley back across the States and sold it. Then I flew to Paris and that's when I ran into you and Sterling Hayden.

I'd tasted Europe and I wanted to go on farther. I didn't want to ever stop traveling.

Milan and Sterling and I spent some effort in Paris, London, and back in the States trying to make a film.

My focus was on Sterling and how he cooperated with the House Un-American Activities Committee and what relationship that had to my own experience with the FBI. Sterling was trying to write about how hashish can save you from alcoholism. The two just never came together. By the end of this experience, I was pretty strung out on a number of drugs, including heroin.

Milan wrote to his father about meeting Sterling.

By now I'm sure that you've finished *The Wanderer* and probably understand why I wanted to make a film about (and with) that man Hayden. The book contains so many things. It enlightened me and it frightened me at the same time. Sterling is brutally honest about himself in that book and, in a way, I wish that I had never read it. It wiped out one of my heroes in one sense and in another sense made him stand even taller in my eyes. I just wish everything wasn't so painful for him.

This from a letter to Milan from Sterling:

You surely know without my saying it that I think of you often, and speak of you often when I wish to impress the locals with the fact that ONCE UPON A TIME I did in fact inhabit a small part of the outer world where such people as Slim came passing by your door while you paced solemnly to and from in front of a teak pilot-house positioned not far from the Quai de Conti, not far from the heart of Paris.

How are you making it? I know all about the surface aspects of what you are doing: you're young and you're strong and you're far from home, but how does it feel inside? What are you finding, in terms – that is – of what you're looking for? Are you having many laughs? Laughs, I was taught long ago by a man named Lawrence Patrick Joseph O'Toole, are the stuff of which life is – or should be – made, but Christ, how hard they are to come by.

That letter was illustrated by Sterling with a sketch of the Paris barge where he and Milan met.

10

NAPLES OR NEPAL?

My pal Doyle Nance basically picked me up and said, "Milan," you're coming with me."

I said, "Where are we going?"

"We're going," and to this day I'm not sure, because of what Doyle knew about geography, and because of Doyle's accent, but I think he said, "We're going to Naples."

I got on the plane with Doyle in a very loaded condition with what money I had left and arrived in Nepal instead of Naples!

I didn't see the first Italian anywhere. There was nothing but Nepalese and trekkers.

I was seriously considering killing myself because I'd been unable to write, I'd been unable to make a living at what I thought was my art, which was writing. I had been unsuccessful at pulling off anything that I thought was revolutionary. I was 29 years old and I just saw the end of my life.

But in Nepal I met Addison Smith and Addison said, "Before you do that, why don't you walk up into the Himalayas for a week and see what happens?"

I walked off for four days with a couple of Sherpas. Of course, Sherpas are born and raised walking in the Himalayas, and these guys insisted I keep up with their pace so they kept feeding me this arak, which was this local moonshine. I slept in my shoes. I just would drop at the end of each day. These guys would go out and wash up and I would just fall down on the floor. We finally arrived at a place called Tachapani (phonetic spelling), which means hot water, there are hot springs there. I climbed in to the hot springs, the first time removing my boots in four days. My feet were so blistered you couldn't distinguish the toes, it just looked all like one big surgical glove. I sat in there just resting for half a day. The Sherpas were long gone by now. They didn't want to wait for this white boy to come along.

There was a Nepalese woman who ran the tavern there and spoke a little English.

She said, "Where you from?"

I said, "I'm from America."

She said, "Oh, I have a friend from America, maybe you know him."

I thought, oh yeah. "What's his name?"

She said, "I don't know, but he wears a purple suit and he has a long hat with a duck's bill out the front of it."

I said, "Wavy Gravy?"

"Yeah, that's him."

That was my first taste of magic in the Himalayas.

I got on up into the mountains and it did so turn my life around that I saw a reason to live. There were the Himalayas to be discovered. There wasn't what had depressed me, what I left behind, but what was before me to investigate and learn about. I decided on that trip to stay among the living and try to live in Nepal.

When I came down from the mountains a friend of mine, Ted Wooster, was leaving Nepal. He's an anthropologist. He said he would rent me his house for six months if I agreed to hire, as a sort of houseboy, his trekking guide.

I said good-bye to Ted and then I turned to my new houseboy. Never having had a houseboy I didn't know quite what to do, but I figured I'd ask him for some tea. He looked at me and, at that moment, we both realized that neither of us spoke one word of the other's language. We were stuck in this house together with no way to communicate, other than to learn one another's language, which we started to do. We did it with symbols and pictures.

We hung a shirt on the wall and I would say to him, "Shirt." He would say to me the word for shirt in Tibetan, and then we would write it on the wall. I hung a pair of pants underneath that and we did pants, and then we drew a face and it wasn't a matter of a week or two we had everything in the house labeled in Tibetan and in English. We labeled phonetically in both languages too.

I went on another trek and realized I really wanted to stay there in Nepal for a long time and learn the language well. In 1972 Mocean's mother came along and we went back to the States.

From Kathmandu, Milan wrote Carl, trying to entice him to come visit and looking for partners in a travel business to introduce Americans to Nepal.

The American Consulate here is very loose – he wrote to Carl – actually good people. Lots of notices on the wall about drugs, mostly with the tone of, "Please don't get caught, we can't help you get out of the bust." God love 'em.

This idea in a letter to Carl in 1972:

I want to send you some musk. As you know, it comes from the musk deer and is used in good perfumes. Good perfume companies will buy it. I would like to smuggle you enough to test the market. I can believe I can buy it for $50 – you can sell for $500.

It is illegal to import it to the States without paying a duty. But it is just a misdemeanor and I can send it in such a way that you can't get popped: addressed to myself in care of you.

So without knowing your reaction, I'm figuring that you might want to dabble in something weird that won't get you hurt. The next package you receive from me (or for me) continue to disassemble until you find the product. Then phone a few perfume companies and ask about their interest, then a price.

Mainly I'm interested in what kind of price you can sell it for so I can determine if it's good to send a bunch.

All this adventuring did not appeal to everyone in Milan's life. In Nepal in April, 1972, he received this handwritten letter from his "Auntie Va" in California – a woman clearly expressing the concerns of many Americans at the time and directing them personally at her nephew. Spelling and punctuation are the late Auntie Va's.

Dear Milan,

This is a beautifull day & I am sitting on my front porch letter writing. Can hear a wood pecker working away on a Redwood tree. Which is a bit stupid if he thinks he can accomplish anything. Just like so many of us who beat our heads on stone walls.

My Dogwood trees are in full bloom & are just beautiful. Had hoped to have the Melvins with me but they were going to Clear Lake yesterday & I haven't heard from them today.

Last Sat. I drove to Jamestown & spent the week end with Gena, coming home on Mon. With my garden in full bloom just now I hate to leave, but my family is so important to me, I go to any one of them who invites me to visit. Gena and I had a nice visit. Wish we lived nearer each other as she won't drive down here & it is too long a trip to do it often.

Haven't seen Janelle for over a month either. Ma & Pa were down two weeks ago today to bring a disgarded mattress for me to give away. We had a pleasant short visit. Don't see them often enough. Having to put Gidget to her rest was hard on all of us. I cried for three days & still can't talk about her. She was such a happy little dog & and gave the entire family lots of happy hours.

I can see absolutely no beauty in the kind of a life Ann & Rudy are living. Being on drugs & welfare is the lazy stupid way of life. Ann has been a liar for so many years she doesn't know what the truth is. Rudy was a nice young man when I first met him but has gone along with Ann & is just as bad. Hard physical work never hurt any one & not one thing is gained in life with out it.

Jack & I worked very hard to build a life for our old age & I heartily disapprove of any & all young people who preffer living on the tax payers money & that is definitely what welfare is.

Milan don't think for one minute you were any sort of a minister. Just seaking piece isn't enough. What you & your generation need is a belief in Christianity. A God that you can believe in, not a cult. Christian, church going people are happy people & they see the Creators hand work all around.

As the saying goes, "Families who pray together, stay together." When adversity hits as it's bound to, they have a higher power than their mere selves to fall back on.

The Melvin curse is my own idea but call it anything you like & the restlessness it produces, especially in the Melvin males, is a curse. Most of it could be controlled if they would be beleave in God & Christ & mature into adults.

Just take stock of your self honey. What have you ever done for your Mother & Father? Don't imagine for one minute that you haven't caused your mother many heartaches, for you have. She loves you as only a Mother can having carried you under her heart for nine months. She will always love you dearly but what have you ever done to cause her to be proud of her Son??

As for your father, he is my brother & I love him dearly. He had to help his father out in the Y. bowling alley when he was only 12 years old to help supplement the family money & hated it. My father was a good family man & his kids could do no wrong but Pop was a poor provider. Friends came first if he had a dollar in his pocket.

I loved my father with a passion but could see his faults many of which he passed on to his son & grandson & you will do likewise if you ever have one. I hope you never do as the Melvin genies will die out. Some things we are born with we seem unable to correct & I guess that is what we inheirit.

I know your Dad does things that I do not approve of & had he been my husband I would have left him years ago. Your Mother is no fool except in that she loves her husband deeply & puts up with his antics as few women would.

Your Mom has raised two thoughtless kids & deserves much more than she has ever received from either. One time I tried to tell your father something about one of you that I didn't like & Your Dad told me "not to meddle in internal affairs" & I have tried to obey.

I think you both would have been happier if more had been expected of you. You kids never wanted for anything & that isn't good.

Milan you are almost thirty – give a year or two, have lived with four women, I don't say was married to you notice, you have no trade or profession & if you don't grow up, buckle down & make something of your self, you will end up as Ann on welfare.

No one hates the war or wants peace more than I do, but your generation just breaks down & destroys things & does nothing to rebuild. The government you all hate has to step in & rebuild, as that is too much work for the Hippies. If they would get in & work through political organizations & clean up our government bureaus we would be better off. Washington is as crooked as any place & needs honesty.

You know Honey learning a few words in several languages isn't going to put bread in your stomach. Get with it man & quit fooling around. It's later than you think.

This hasn't been a happy letter to write nor an easy one. That is why it has taken me so long to answer yours of Jan 24. If I didn't love you & know of your potentials I wouldn't give a darn how you live, but you are part of my family. A family I love dearly.

As for your Mother greeting you with open arms, have you ever greeted her that way? Your Mothers parents were both from Norway as was my mother. They are a cold nation, having to work hard & fight for what they needed. Affection wasn't neccessary or part of their make up but loyalty was.

Your parents would never think to tell you you were waisting your most productive years but you are. Make up your mind to do something that they will be proud of. When ever you call them on the phone the heavens open up & they are elated. Do something more concrete than picking up the receiver & calling them.

I don't know whether you are a longhair or not but hope you are not. The new mens style is most attractive & would look well on you. Your Ma hated your longhair but did tell me you at least kept it clean.

I still have letters you wrote me when you lived in Willits & I bribed you to go to the dentist with the promise of a pair of guns and a holster. That was wrong of me.

Will close for now, hoping just one of my twenty-six nieces & nephews would live close by to give me a hand occassionally as the years pile on.

Much love and good wishes for your future,

Auntie Va

Milan's files bulged with his letters home to his family. Some were crisis appeals for funds, like this from early 1972.

Dear Dad,

I've thought a lot since my last letter and I've decided to ask you to loan me the money for a camera. The sum I need to get a camera and lenses is a stiff one, I'm afraid it will take $150.

Peter just wrote me and said he had cleaned and repaired my camera. So when I get it back I'll sell it and repay you. Sound okay?

Others were traditional, asking for news from home and expressing some homesickness even as he wanted to travel on. This Western Union telegram went home to his mother that same year:

HAPPIEST OF BIRTHDAYS TO YOU STOP WISH I WAS THERE WITH YOU LOVE MILAN

There were jokes mixed in with requests for help on the road.

Dear Mom,

A short note about the package. Please send it air mail or air freight. I'm sorry about the expense of sending it by air, but sea mail takes 3 - 4 months and chances are slim of it getting through.

In any case, please hurry – the seat is beginning to wear out on this pair of Levis and I'm starting to look like a hippy.

Love,

Milan

There were life updates.

Dear Folks,

A quick line to let you know that the son and heir is on the tropical island of Ceylon. How and why I ended up here can all be explained in terms of a love affair.

Julian West is her name. I met her in Nepal, spent some time together there, then arranged to meet in India which we did about two weeks ago. Anyway, we're here to finish up some of her business, then I hope to bring her back to the States with me for a few months.

I can't tell you much about Ceylon yet because I've been here only 36 hours. I'll write again when I have had a little time to nose around the island. But for sure there are beaches, tanning skies, and fabulous under-water coral gardens frequented by all those tropical fish that can be seen only in aquariums in the States.

Right now I'm trying to make arrangements for a little beach house where I can live for the next month and finish the work I have to do for this language book idea. I'll return to the States loaded with materials to show a literary agent and publisher.

In the meantime please know that your son and brother is spending most of his time underwater playing with the fish, or on the beach playing with Julian, or at the desk playing with words.

I have an address and would appreciate a quick card from you so I can be sure that you have received this and know that I am still sound of body and romantic of mind.

Love to you – I'll write again soon. Milan

There were poetic laments to his friends Carl and Allison.

... add to a Harley 74 and a Winchester 73, a Corona 100 and you will have the sum total of everything that I need that I do not now possess – excluding, of course, one large-brown-eyed California girl that I had no right to request.

You will excuse a temporarily drunken Uncle Travel for his plunge into the muddle of melancholy and melodrama. But I need that particular girl in my life, and yet I can see no way in which that might be possible, considering the needs and temperaments of each of us. I will, of course, write her – as I have thousands of times in my daily flashes and approximately twenty times in real life. Each time I write her a letter the size of it shrinks measurably. In the beginning it bordered on a novelette, in the end it was one sentence. In all cases I refused to mail them, probably because I feared rejection in the form of a sensible reply and definitely because I simply did not know how to say what I felt – and still don't for that matter. I do know, however, that she must record music and present it to the public, and further, that I must travel to every corner of the world in order to make sure that the particular demons which haunt me are to be found only in my own head and not tucked away in some underbrush of a damp jungle or some lip-cracking dark cave aside a mountain.

Speaking of a Winchester 73, I have enclosed a photograph printed just a few days ago here in Asia. The photographer is an old Nepali that snapped this trekking permit photo with an ancient machine long overdue for the Smithsonian. The old box has no shutter. Instead, the lens is covered with a bottle cap which the old gentleman removes (when the subject has adjusted his pose) and then waves about in the air with his own magical twist, and then replaces.

Speaking of a Corona 100, I feel a book coming on, a book of photographs and languages. I have recently discovered in myself a facility for languages and wish to share it. In the noblest of terms it will ever so slightly promote the development of this global village which I see emerging. On the lowest level, it might put a few rupees in my pocket, thereby allowing my own travel and education to continue.

I have consumed Tibetan at a rate that surprised me, sacrificing all personal pride in order to learn the language. I got into some incredible jams bargaining for things that I did not want, prostrating myself in front of cranky lamas, starting brawls in the chang houses, and masquerading as a Tibetan. But it worked. It's in my head and down on paper in an orderly, understandable form.

The book will contain a collection of Arabic, Tibetan, Nepali, Afghani, Hindu, Spanish, and French. I see it as a combination of the very academic grammar books and the cheapo-tourist "Where is the toilet"-type books, containing the best of each and avoiding the rest. The purpose of it is to involve the reader's emotions by getting him into the streets armed with a formula of sentence construction and enough words to be able to learn more. God willing! More of this later.

I will now retire to my one-handed love affair.

Love,

Milan

Technology was slower back then, as this fragment points out.

How far out it was to really talk to you, Carl. Both of us sounded flabbergasted. But it did rearrange my perspective because I still am "only a phone call away." For a while there I thought I was in the fourteenth century and America hadn't been discovered yet. One feels very distant in time and space after all this time in the desert. The conversation brought me back home a bit and it feels good.

When Milan and Carl were working on a film project, this reflection in a letter from Milan regarding what he was doing and why.

I've detected a pattern in my life of wandering and that's to tiptoe into a new place, suss out the powers running the politics and business, and connect with them as a "big timer from the West." Most of the time I live with the common folk, in their way, because that's really what it's all about. But these other connections to power will be valuable if we want to do projects in their various kingdoms.

This letter, written during the same period as Auntie Va's assault, from Milan to "Mom and Pop" Melvin provides more counterpoint.

As of this writing it is still a few days before Christmas. But Christmas never comes to this place like it does to your house, so we'll probably barely feel it this year. Bonnie and I do sit here and muse about how you all will spend it, and how we will spend it. Anyway, by the time you get this note you will have already spent it.   We received a nice card and note from Auntie Gena. She enclosed a few photos that you took of each other back in '69. It made me realize that I have no photos of you over here. What a sweetheart Auntie Gena is. What sweethearts you will be if you send me a photo or two of you. Everybody here wants to know what you look like and I'd like to look at what you look like. OK?

The letter continues with details about the beginnings of Milan's trading business and his plan for a vacation.

I need this rest. It's been nine months of hard work.

On January 2nd we charge off on another adventure. A pilgrimage to India, for 15 days only.

He wanted to hear the Dalai Lama speak at Bodh Gaya.

No telling how many people will be there, but it looks like hundreds of thousands. I chartered a bus (owned by the Khampa Army – the guerrillas) and filled it with all the Tibetans that I do business with. We'll pile into the bus early on the morning of January 2nd and stay locked together until we return on or about the 17th of January. The bus is a big one, 56 seats, and only four of us are Westerners – the rest all Tibetans. We'll be taking a huge, brightly decorated Tibetan tent with us. Think of us on that morning.

When we get back we jump right into the nursery project. The building itself is complete. All the walls, windows, and doors are in place, with remarkable accuracy for Asia. Bonnie will use the nursery room for a school room until we can construct the school room.

I'm using the same system I used to raise the batch of money that built the nursery room: send a letter to everyone I know asking them for a donation. Last time I requested $10 per person, but this time we've got it up to $20. Can you chip in, too?

Other than that? Our plan is to stay here until May or early June. Then we'll decide whether we make a swing to America or just head south to the South Sea Islands.

I'll write upon return from India. You'll probably get it in late January.

Be well and don't forget the photos.

Love, Milan

Later he urged them to come visit him in Kathmandu.

The house is huge, made of handmade bricks and has intricately carved wooden windows done in ancient Newari style, wooden beams for ceilings, mudded floors and whitewashed inside walls. The main building is two floors (or three if you count the attic, which is beautiful), with about 12 rooms, not counting the hallways or the 3 or 4 kitchens. Joined to the main house by archways are two smaller brick buildings of 2 or 3 rooms each that are servants' quarters.

Outside the courtyard is an orchard that surrounds the whole place on three sides and a brick wall that goes all the way around to keep the goats, sheep, and cattle out.

Everywhere are the signs of I don't know how many years of probably pretty good living. The wooden ladder-stairs that connect the three floors are worn smooth by millions of ascensions, the outer diameter of the well, rounded by many bellies leaning against it as the folks pulled the water up.

My house is located just a few hundred yards across the rice fields from the Buddhist Stupa called Boudha Nath. There it glows outside my bedroom windows at sunset and sunrise. The Stupa is very tall, probably 10 stories or so, made of whitewashed earth and cement, crowned with another four stories of golden metal. On each of the four sides of the top piece are painted the "compassionate eyes of Buddha" facing each of the cardinal directions. The base of the Stupa is round, covering about a city block. There is a stone and earth walkway going around it and the whole works is surrounded by old-style buildings occupied by Tibetans who spread their wares out each day in hopes of catching the tourists' eyes.

Tourists of all nationalities visit the Stupa during the daylight hours. But the nights are reserved for Tibetans (and us "locals"). Sometimes brightly nyloned Japanese come, sometimes Europeans, and occasionally, like yesterday, a truckload of Chinese dressed in Mao threads and buttons. We tried to talk to them, but their leaders said, "Oh, no! Oh, no!"

At sunset each night the walkway around the Stupa looks like Madison Avenue at lunch time, only the folks are all Tibetan making khora, walking round and round the Stupa clockwise and spinning the prayer wheels or prostrating their way around by lying down, marking the place where their forehead touched with a conch shell, then standing up, moving their feet up to where the shell is, picking up the shell and prostrating themselves again and on and on around the Stupa. Whew!

One of the first Christian missionaries to reach Tibet, a very pompous

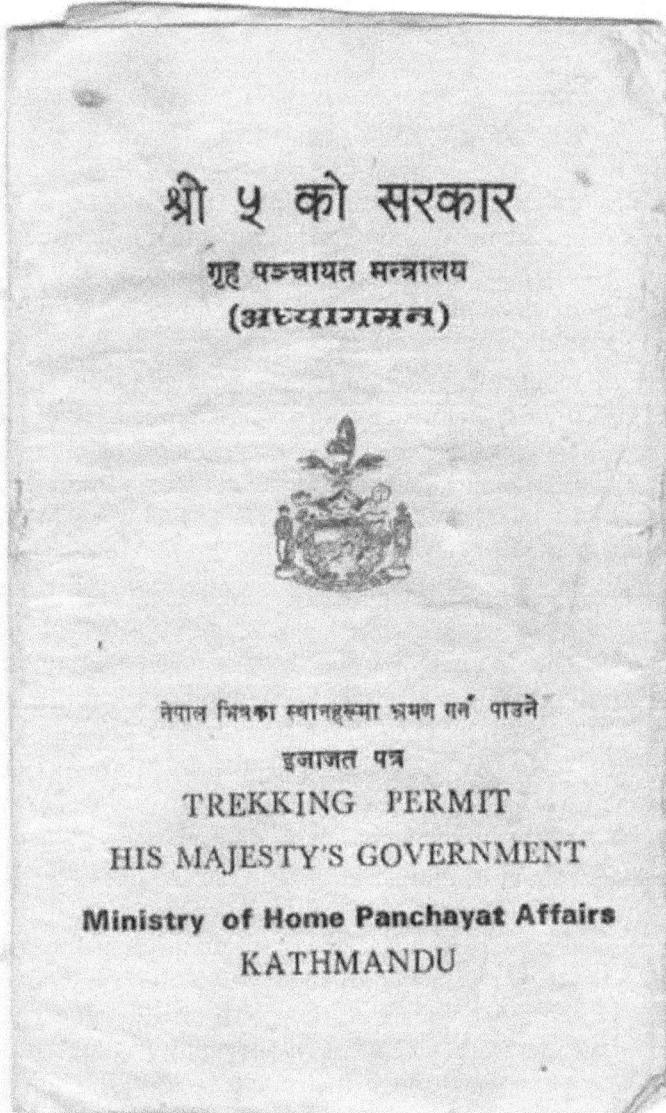

श्री ५ को सरकार

गृह पञ्चायत मन्त्रालय

(अध्यागमन)

नेपाल भित्रका स्थानहरूमा भ्रमण गर्ने पाउने

इजाजत पत्र

TREKKING PERMIT

HIS MAJESTY'S GOVERNMENT

Ministry of Home Panchayat Affairs

KATHMANDU

but super devout cat named Desideri, wrote, "I was ashamed to have a heart so hard that I did not honor my Master as these people do their deceiver." Even being so bent on converting these "heathens," the jealous Jesuit recorded a devotion the likes of which he had never experienced.

But what can I say on notebook scribblings that would do it justice? Like the best of moments, you gotta be here!!

Please folks, do figure an excuse to come visit. I am making extensive investigations into the black market to see if there is any way in which you might be able to make the journey for free.

Love to you,

Milan

This letter was to friends in the States regarding a trek in the Himalayas.

Lang Tang valley is due north of Kathmandu, a disappointing trek. The trail is overused by Westerners (or foreigners). It rained like hell almost every day. The leeches were out in full force, the once strong culture has been watered down by all the contact with outsiders. The prices on food rivaled those of America.

Usually the monsoons peter out by mid-September, but this year they hung on until the day before yesterday, mid-October. For our walk that meant that the mountains were always shrouded in clouds and the leeches were all too plentiful. The first day out we encountered rain. We are experienced Himalayan trekkers and we had all our rain gear in our packs. Unfortunately, the rain gear was at the bottom of our packs and by the time we dug it out our boots, socks and ankles were literally covered with leeches, hungry ones.

Panic set in, couldn't help it. We kicked, stomped, and shook trying to get them off, to no avail. As we picked them off, more came. Finally, we broke into a run, laughing (a little too hysterically), heading for a hut at the top of the ridge. We reached it and ducked inside just ahead of a Nepali woman with a boy at her side and a baby on her back. All were covered with the little beasts.

She was cool about it, though. A third of her life has been spent in the company of leeches. She nonchalantly scraped them off with a scythe. The next three days were reruns of the first, minus the panic. We came to spot the leeches early and snatch them off before they hit food: us. Finally we got above the 9,000 foot elevation, into territory too cold for the leeches, and all was well (except for that nagging feeling that we would have to hike back down through their niche again). The animals in the lowlands have it much tougher than we creatures with hands and leather packages on our feet. The leech hits them while they are grazing. He inches his way over the tough hide to softer places. eyes, ears, noses and assholes, cocks and cunts, that's where they lodge. It's sickening to see a helpless cow with blood pouring from every orifice. Fortunately, the monsoons have disappeared until about next June, with them the leeches.

I will never go trekking during monsoons again.

Milan sent piles of letters back to the States, showing off – as he himself characterized it – his amazing adventures. These were letters he copied, expecting to use for future works.

Late April 1972

Dear Carl and Allison:

I aim to brag in this here letter of the times we had in the Himalayas. Hemingway got nothing on me in any of his "adventures" or his ability to tell stories in single syllables and half sentences.

We left Kathmandu with a rotten set of papers and high hopes of shucking our way into what we knew was a forbidden territory. We were five: Susan, an American woman, Addison, the hipster's mark trail, two Tibetan brothers, Gonpo and Namgyal, and me. A short plane ride took us to Gurkha, which is only an airstrip along the Marsyandi River; no people, no town, and when the plane departed there was no way to tell that it had ever been there or that it would ever come again.

There was one other man besides ourselves that got off the plane in Gurkha, a Tibetan man whose legs were pumping before we even touched ground. Out of the plane he leaped, made a quick left face and strode off north. We figured he was our man and we headed after him, catching up with him only because he had to wait for a dugout to ferry him across the river. His directions were to stay along the edge of this river until we reached our destination, the Nye-Shang Valley. "Police?" Yes, there were police and Nepali Army, about 100 of them at the last check post in Chame. He invited us to come to his house, should we make it; he would go ahead and meet us there.

It's weird to walk under baking skies with forty new pounds on your back, not knowing whether you'll be able to reach your destination without being turned back and forced to retrace your steps through that heat. All along the trail we disguise our real goal, saying that we are only going to the next village up the river. There were some diversions, though, like blisters, raw spots where your pack rubs before you can discover them and readjust your straps. Also, there is a wonderful Nepali custom resembling the McCoy-Hatfield feuds where two angry men will stand on the tops of knolls and shout back and forth curses that sounded like, "You're a cocksucker and an eyesore around these parts." Here in the lowlands the fleas and mosquitos keep you busy at night too.

The third morning out we got our first glimpse of the mountains that we are hoping to walk around and behind, the Annapurna Himal. It never seems as far as it always is. These nights in the lowlands we eat and sleep in Nepali houses. By day we share the trail with scores of Tibetan folks that are on their way back up to the Nye-Shang Valley now that the winter is over. Most are women carrying eighty pounds plus – the year's supply of provisions. The loads include children and crippled old people probably making their last return. We asked about their men and were told that they were off to Hong Kong, Singapore and the Philippines trading. It seems that the people from this valley are the only people under Nepali control that are granted passports to leave the country. They were granted this concession by the former king because they claimed they couldn't grow enough food on their rocky land to support themselves, but, also because their land is so close to the Chinese border (Tibet) that the king wanted a little insurance against Chinese flirtation.

The fourth day out we met a brown-eyed handsome man named Tashi. We hung out with him all day and told him of our real plans. He gave us a complete description of what was ahead: another two days' walk would get us to Chame, the last Nepali outpost, where 100 Gurkha rifles guarded a narrow canyon. Every "Ingie" that went up there was turned back he said, but, for thirty rupees per man he would sneak us around the barracks... our first ace! We more or less agreed to the plan but said we would try jiving our way through first.

We all stayed together for the next day, too, sleeping in a big bhati with several other folks that night. Among them was one Nepali "reading man" who was on his way to Chame to begin work with the soldiers. He was very uncomfortable because we were nearing Tibetan culture, he was the only Nepali in the house, and Tashi and a few of his outlaw partners were putting him on horribly, zipping him up into his nylon jacket, rolling him around the floor and forcing "arak" (like saki) down his throat.

The next afternoon we reached Tashi's village, a small one of three stone houses next to a meadow. The altitude here is high enough to graze "Dzomo" (half yak, half cow) herds (9,000 ft. or so). There are also horses and mules that belong to the Khampa Army fellows who live in the five tents around the edge of the meadow. Towards dusk the meadow fills up with 60 or 70 of the Tibetans that we have been walking along the trail with. Dinner is finished and the boogie begins: dancing and singing around a huge bonfire. Tashi is obviously the man here too, creaming us and the Tibetan pomos alike with his songs and steps. At one point he even slowed the pace and let us "Ingies" take a few lessons, which created a lot of laughter, but also copped us many invitations to stay in people's houses up in Nye-Shang (again, if we can get through).

The following day we played in the meadow and the snow on the mountainsides, washed our clothes, raced the horses, took photographs, and spent a good deal of the time lamenting the fact that we have probably carried all this cold weather gear through all those lowland days for nothing. We are all depressed. Chame, the check post, is only four hours up the trail. We are anxious to have it out with the army, but nobody wants to hear the refusal.

Sure enough! We reach Chame the next noon and are given an immediate refusal before we can even employ any of the riffs we have worked out in front. So we decide to hang around a day or two, in hopes of what, nobody knew. We spent our time trying to make friends among the soldiers, trying to find out who the head man is and getting an audience with him. Or, at least, hoping that if we get caught trying to sneak around the post that it will be by one of the hamburgers that we played volleyball with, or cards, or got drunk with, or gave cigarettes to.

A day and half later we did work our way into the top cop's office. He explained that beyond his outpost there were no Nepali police, only "those Tibetans," therefore he could not offer our band any "protection" from them. We had to swallow our reaction to that and begin our smiling lies about how the Kathmandu office had said that we could go onward with these very papers – he didn't go for it – we pleaded, recount out expenses – he sat unmoved – I tried a 200-rupee bribe – he stood up outraged – I tried crying (which was easy to do) and he threw us out. For some reason, though, during the course of the conversation he said that Susan's papers were in order and that she and the two Tibetans could continue onward, but, that Addison and I could not. I'm sure that this was a half-assed way out of the argument, thinking that she would not go on without us. We took him at his word, held an overly public good-bye ceremony in front of the whole regiment, which had become interested in our case by now, whispered a rendezvous to each other, and Addison and I headed back down the trial looking as dejected as we could.

Back down to Tashi's village, where we found him, completed our contract and fell to organizing our midnight creep. The whole village (all Tibetan refugees) joined the conspiracy. This kind of stuff was every day to these people for most of their lives so they enjoyed the intrigue and helped us out by feeding us, bedding us down until moonrise and giving us little aids like walking sticks and dark cloth to cover our day-glow backpacks.

The moon came and we went, back up the trail, right up to the volleyball court which is in the front yard of the barracks. We can hear the soldiers inside talking, Addison whispers, "It's us against 100 Gurkha rifles."

I think we're busted because they can hear my heart trying to crash its way out of my chest. We keep crawling.

"Tashi, you promised us a different trail!"

"Yes," he says, "It's on the other side of the barracks."

How do you say "terrific!" in Tibetan?

There was another trail, catch that, once upon a time there was another trail. Now it's a place of avalanches and felled forests, where we walked suspended ten feet above the ground and where water-soaked landslides live. But it was only two hours of scrambling and we reached Tashi's pal's house. It all seemed so silly and simple then. Tashi's friend, his old lady, and eight young Tibetan women slept cuddled around the fire; his friend got up, made tea and fed us while Tashi harassed all the sleeping pomos by stuffing pine branches down in their blankets, coloring their noses black with charcoal and tying their braids together. It must have been a funny sight when everyone woke up in the morning. We didn't wait to see it, we were gone before dawn, feeling good! It is April Fool's Day. Thank you, Tashi, hope to see you again.

Two hours up the trail we reach a bridge across the river. It's a bridge guarded by the Khampa Army, the Dalai Lama's Army, still maneuvering in and out of Tibet proper in hopes of one day returning home. As we cross the bridge we realize that this is a definite line, there are no Nepalis up here, "only those Tibetans" and they sure look fine. It feels like home. We even meet Susan, Namgyal, and Gonpo as planned. Now we are actually in the Nye-Shang Valley, a long corridor of ten or twelve miles in length, flat, elevation 12,000 feet, stuck between the Annapurna Himal (in case you still have that atlas) and some other range to the north. As we settle in to some of those invitations we realize a lot of other things, too. The map we have is completely wrong, based probably on aerial photographs. Obviously, whoever drew it up had never really been here.

We see why the Nepali government does not want foreigners up here, and that's because it's truly a third nation, neither Nepal nor China's Tibet, but a twenty-five-mile wide strip that apparently stretches the length of the border between the other two nations. "Bhotis" the people call themselves and they let their land be policed by the Khampa Army, but there seems to be little need of any "keeping of the peace."

The first village in Nye-Shang that we stayed in was called Bagba by the people that lived there and some other name by the chump that made up the map names. It's a cliff dwelling-type of village, built high above the valley floor, near some not so steep mountainsides that have been terraced over the years. We began to understand why these people have to rely on trading and smuggling for a living; crops can be grown during four months of the year only and then the space is limited, confined to a few hillsides and the river bed which is mainly boulders. The only vegetable matter available for compost is pine needles and damn little of that since most villages are above the tree line, and the altitude limits the plants that can be grown to potatoes, grains, turnips, and two green leafy things that we never could identify because we only saw it in its dried form from last year's crop. They do have some meat but, since Buddhists may not kill, an animal must die of old age or have an "accident." The land is so barren that it cannot even support yaks, that high-altitude buffalo that can survive on almost nothing. Boulders and mountains is what Nye-Shang is

all about.

We stayed in the village for three weeks moving back and forth among all six villages. In each place we were given places to call our own, in some cases it was people's altar rooms full of pictures of the Dalai Lama, Karmapa, or other Buddhist heavies. In other cases we were given a whole house while the folks were out of town.

All the houses were built on the same pattern: an open, or half-open courtyard downstairs where the "dee" (more of them later) were kept, the courtyard is floored with pine needles which these sort-of-cows shit on and trample into a compost/fertilizer. There was always a covered balcony above where grains were kept dry and living rooms (usually no more than two) were off these balconies.

The photos I took will show you better than this letter (they are on their way to you now).

Our hygiene was always difficult. A harsh, super cold wind was blowing whenever it wasn't snowing and the only water trickled off glaciers just a few hundred feet up the mountains, the result was frozen noses and hands every time we tried to wash up. The body lice seemed to find our company quite agreeable, though, for they did quite well and happily multiplied. These "dees," which are the sickliest-looking mutation of a cow that I ever saw were weird too. When we would go down into the courtyards to take our morning crap they would crowd around, edging to within a few inches of your face, waiting for the turd to drop from your ass so they could scarf it up. I never saw a shit-eating cow before! Also, all those things that happen to people that are not bred in high altitudes happened to us: the lips crack and split, the nose runs full time, the hair dries out, and a red glow/burn grabs your face.

Every time we move from one village to the next we draw huge crowds, mostly children, who watch our every move. Susan may be able to claim that she was the first Western woman ever to visit this valley. We heard no reports of any previous. Addison and I would get reactions approaching those received by Elvis whenever we said anything.

Whenever we weren't in our sleeping bags or hunched around a fire we were out visiting old monasteries, gompas. They were always full of images, some a full story in height, drums, trumpets eight feet long, paintings, ancient holy books, and thousands of other types of random paraphernalia. In one gompa was a special room full of weapons that, I swear, dated back to Ghengis Khan as well as the moguls, the British India, and World War Two. There were spears, swords, arrows, matchlock rifles, bayonets, and weird beheaders. In all cases they were bathed in butter and had a scarf tied around some part of them to indicate that they had been captured by the Dharma, never to be used against men or animals again.

As I read this over it seems like a long list of hardships but it didn't seem so bad at this time. The people of Nye-Shang more than compensated for the discomforts; they gave us their houses, firewood, water, cooking gear to fill out our meager kit and when they didn't just give us food they sold it to us at local prices. We nosed around in their lives without putting them uptight and they opened up to us completely, stopping work to show us about and make us at home. We bought some few things from them but there was not too much treasure to be found since most of it had already been carried off to the markets of Southeast Asia.

Towards the end of our stay in Nye-Shang we got the worries about our exit. We would sit around the fire at meal times, usually as drunk as we could make ourselves, and discuss the next step. Nobody wanted to try to re-sneak the post at Chame, the pass to the west was still closed by snow so we decided to go north, hope for a lucky day and try to get over a 17,700-foot pass and down to Muktinath. Anyway we went we still had to sneak past one check post or another back into the official Nepal. If we took this pass, called Thorong La, we could go to that place I wrote you about before, Muktinath, the pilgrimage place where Hindus and Buddhists alike go to pray for release from similar incarnations in the future, the place where 108 springs of water and two spouts of fire come from the same rocks.

While still in Nye-Shang we tried to get as much information as possible about the pass and we got reactions ranging from "Six people died up there last year," to "When you go that high it makes your heart beat too fast, your lungs burn and your head ache. Why do you want to do that?" to "You candy-ass gringos, quit talking so much and get your asses up there!" Most people suggested taking a guide of some sort since the snow had obscured the trail, so we found a goat herder who was willing to take us with him on his trip over. Then he split all of a sudden and we jammed up the trail, completely unprepared, in hopes of catching him.

It's a day and a half's walk from the valley, over the pass and down to Muktinath, and you have to carry all your provisions because there is only one unoccupied cabin between the two places and no food or wood. We were still an hour or so from this cabin when a snow storm rolled up the canyon after us. It was impossible to turn back so we pushed on and slipped into the yak herder's cabin just in time. No one was home, but there was a half a day's wood in the corner. Still, we all dropped our packs and scrambled outside to gather all the juniper scrub that we could – just in case. It snowed most of the night but the morning was clear and bright with six inches of snow that stayed on the ground (the color slides of this should be nice, you'll see them before I will).

Namgyal and Gonpo decided to go back down the canyon to Nye-Shang to score food and wood – just in case. They were gone about two hours when another blizzard hit and we knew for sure that they would not be coming back that day. So, we settled in: I carved some dice, Addison, Susan, and I sat around the fire playing Razzle-Dazzle and making a lot of death jokes while it snowed all day. About nine o'clock that night Namgyal and Gonpo came crashing through the doorway covered with snow, their pants so frozen that they could hardly bend their knees. They had walked seven hours with that blizzard at their backs in order to get the food and wood back to us. The snow stopped a short while after they arrived and we all spent the coldest night of our lives. Everybody wearing every piece of clothes they had inside the sleeping bags and still no one slept for the cold. Strange things happen to your body at an altitude like that in a cold that cold, among them is a strike by your bladder requiring you to piss every ten minutes, eventually you just let it go down your leg just for the few seconds of warmth that it gives your thighs.

The next morning we discover that the trails either up to the pass or back down to the valley are totally snowed under, but the sun is shining brightly so we pile back into the cabin, ration out our food and wood, play craps this time and talk about the people we all know in California. The roof leaked badly as the sun melted the snow so we had to move the crap game around a lot, the dice got muddy, we got muddy, but everybody was so dirty by this time that no one gave it a second thought. That night was not quite so cold.

Next morning we made a stack of Tibetan breads and were trying to wash the dice off in the snow when two other Tibetans arrived on their way over the pass. We fed them, begged permission to join them, packed hurriedly, and slid our way behind our new friends as well as we could. When I was riding that Harley through the rain in Spain all I had was a pair of cowboy boots, this time, climbing a 17,000-foot pass all I had was smooth bottom motorcycle boots. Just once in my life I would like to feel prepared. Most of the trail up to the top we were crotch deep in snow, so we all had to learn to walk again: withdraw your leg from your last step, throw it as far out in front of you as you can, and slam your nuts down against the ice again. Finally, at about 5:30 we reached the top and beheld the world from a whole new angle. It was getting late but, no one wanted to leave. We planted prayer flags, took photos, threw snowballs, gooned in the snow and all manner of other giddy foolery inspired by the rare air, I'm sure.

The Tibetans reminded us that we had to drop down to an elevation of 12,000 feet before we would reach Muktinath and the sun had already sunk. Those following three hours we spent mostly on our faces and if we were lucky, on our asses, half falling, half skiing, most of it in pitch blackness with only the vague form of the man ahead of you to follow. We were all absolutely exhausted and punchy and giggling and too fucked up to feel the pain. When we eventually reached Muktinath the only Bhati in the area thought we were bandits. Who else would arrive at an hour like that unless they were doing something out of line? Finally they took us in for food and a few hours' sleep. In the morning nobody recognized his own body nor could anyone remember receiving such a beating the previous day. We did, however get it together to pray at the springs of fire and water. There were naked Sadhus there in the freezing early hours splashing through the fountains.

So, here we were, about to sneak around another check post, this one a veritable fortress, back into Nepal, with no plan. We went as near as we dared, ducked into a house and waited for dark again. We all got super drunk again, this time with an old smuggler who volunteered to lead us by night to the edge of Jomosom, the outpost. From there we were on our own, which he did. Our reasoning was that if we could get into the town and kick around for a few minutes we could claim we came up from the south and got lost in town. We reached the town, no one appeared to be awake so we crept across the bridge and past the main check post and that's when we discovered that we were standing in a narrow lane between two very long rows of barracks. Without anybody saying anything it was plain to see that everyone felt, "Aw, fuck 'em. The worst they can do is throw us out of the country." So we half-strode and half-tiptoed on down the line; at the end of the third and last set of barracks we heard a surprised "Ko Ho?" (Nepali "Who goes there?") Addison and I both unleashed a string of "Oh, boy!" and "Are we glad to see you!" and "Where is a hotel?" etc., etc. Apparently it so confused him that he just pointed south in the direction that we were headed, we thanked him and skipped back into legality.

From there on it was downhill most of the way with a hot springs at Tatopani in which we soaked for two days and literally rolled huge sheets of dirt off our skin. This trail is the Jomosom to Pokhara Trail, but last time I was so impressed with this walk: this time it seemed so diminished and run of the mill. We made it to Pokhara without incident. But there was a growing silence among us and lots of arguments flared up with the Nepali people over food and prices. We called it the "Tibetan Comedowns," a bizarre form of cultural shock, reentry mind bends. A night in the Tibetan refugee camp in Pokhara, where we stayed with family of Gonpo and Namgyal, somewhat eased the shock.

But the next morning we were on an eleven-hour bus ride back to Kathmandu, definitely Nepal! Kathmandu ("Please give me one Rupee, I have no mother, no father, and no air condish") was our second shock: pavement, strange smells, and a city pace. I'm not comfortable here now: the insects, the still heat, the vegetables that rot before you can get them home to cook, the visa that has run out. When you know what it can be like, it's hard to settle for less. Which brings me to the close of this word omelet, written to you as well as me for later review.

Today I received your letter dated the anniversary of the first shot fired at Lexington, loaded with news, it was! First reaction: thank you for the loan, as of this date, 2 May, I have not yet seen my name in the book at the bank. One more favor please, call the bank and say that I have not received the bread and demand that they send a cable to the Nepal Bank Ltd. inquiring into the reasons. Probably an emergency lie would help (which is almost the case). Sometimes the banks here in Asia hold the bread for long periods of time for their own investment use but an irate word from home usually moves them. Will cable upon receipt. Really sorry about the Moroccan adventure cancellation, could have been fun for all.

Ah, yes, photos. Within a week or two you should receive by mail five or six rolls of color film that I shot on this last reconnaissance mission. In order to save a little bread I bought some out of date stock, and wished later that I hadn't. Please rush it to a developer and have it made into slides, it will give you some idea of where I was, even though the color film ran out before we reached the best places and the high pass. There is a definite order to the photos, starting with the greens of the lowlands and finishing with the quiet browns and grays of the Nye-Shang area. There should be a photo of our pal Tashi (the one who snuck around the Chame post), you can identify him by the pink ribbon in his hair. Don't show this picture to any Moguls, they might want to ship him to stardom and we both know what that would do.

This brings me to this very moment and I'm sure that I'm not sure about that. The only money I have is yours, which hasn't arrived yet. My options are many, my information incomplete. I feel I must learn one more language before I return. For this I will go west to Afghanistan or south and east to Bali, Indonesia. On the periphery lingers the possibility to move north and a little west to the high plateaus above the oncoming monsoons, to places where "Ingies" have never been. Again, the morning of departure will decide the direction, as always I am in touch with you.

I love you and miss you very much just now...

Milan

P.S. "Muckeye good; see you tomato sauce," we say around here.

Another letter home set the scene at mail call.

Early June 1972

Dear   Dad,
Mom   and
Sister J:

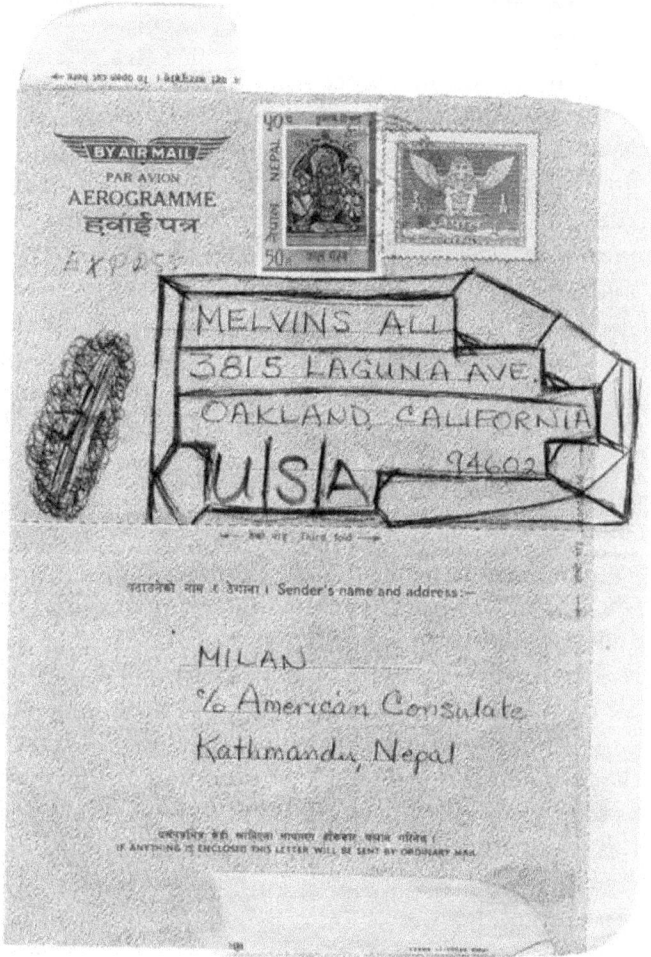

Here's a couple of things for the "unbelievable" list. First, I'm still in Kathmandu, and second and most important THE PACKAGE ARRIVED! Three months and a week or so. Across America by truck, onto the Atlantic and around the horn by ship, across the Indian Continent by God-only-knows-what-means, and into the Nepali Foreign Post Office just like it was supposed to happen. I mean, "I couldn't believe!" and neither could anyone else around town that saw me step out of the Post Office lavatory looking like the proverbial mild-mannered reporter for a great Metropolitan newspaper dressed in dark blue Levis, matching shirt, eating dried apricots, reading "God Bless You, Mr. Rosewater" and playing with a yo-yo. (It was too hot to wear the socks or I would have put both pair on immediately.) THANK YOU, THANK YOU, THANK YOU – to you (as well as any one of the fast-fingered dock workers and slight-of-hand artists, called Postal Employees that might have snatched the package but didn't). REALLY AMAZING.

The scene in the customs office that I had to go through before they would let me have my stuff was a funny one. There were four of us foreigners (all Americans) in there at the same time getting packages: a tycoon from Texas wearing an alligator golf T-shirt and draped in cameras, the pregnant wife of a visiting college professor wearing a loose dress around a massive belly, and a Methodist missionary wearing the beatific smile of the Lord and this young lad wearing very old and often patched Levis. All four of us grinning as hard as we could as we lied through our teeth about the value of the contents of our respective packages. "Purano, Purano. Yo purano ho," we were all saying in broken Nepali, meaning, "Old, old stuff. Not worth a damn, any of it. I don't even care if I pick this stuff up or not, useless garbage," we all lied, as our knees trembled and our hands shook in anticipation of actually capturing these goods of ours.

I explained that my package was a "cruel joke on the part of my mother who had disowned me and thrown me out of the house years ago, then had me arrested and thrown into jail just before they deported me. The pants I had left with her to wash, which she didn't do for years, waiting for me to outgrow them. The shirts were old rags that I used to clean my car with, the fruit would probably be rotten, the vitamin pills poison, the books were mostly likely of a religious nature (which I didn't need), the socks she knew I couldn't use in this heat and the yo-yos were included as a sideways crack that she thought I had lost my mind for good." Anyway, it worked. I got away with a customs bill of 6.43 Rupees (64 cents American).

After the episode was over the four of us met in the street to find out how each other had fared. Everyone made out in direct proportion to his lie. The Texan saw little difference between his performance in the Post Office and doing business in his home state, the mother-to-be was somewhat embarrassed about the size of the tale she had told, the missionary considered it God's work that he was saving money for his supporting congregation back home, and I was pleased with my own imagination for coming up with such vivid details on the spot and already beginning to compose the letter that I am now writing to you. It just goes to prove – what, I cannot say.

Really, everything is perfect. I gave the two yo-yos to the 10-year-old and 6-year-old Tibetan boys living here in the house and they are just now beginning to catch on. Nobody has seen a yo-yo in this part of the world EVER – magic, pure fall-from-the-sky magic.

I'm leaving Kathmandu, though, definitely within ten days, which may sound suspect, I know, because I only came here for two weeks in the first place, and that was over eight months ago. But really, tomorrow morning I make plane reservations for Calcutta, India. When I reach Calcutta I will be able to determine which way the "powers that be" will allow me to return to the good ole USA.

As I said in my last letter, I want to go East via Indonesia so I can pick up another language. But it seems that there are several requirements that I must meet, if I plan to travel East. Among them are: $500 which you have to show before they let you off the airplane (I have only a little more than half that amount), an "onward" plane ticket that guarantees whatever government that you won't get stranded in their country (which I don't have) and short hair (which I don't have, but which I might adopt if necessary). The old romantic days of a man working his way around the world are finished and I sometimes find myself cursing this century in which I was born and hoping somehow to discover a time machine that would take us all back to the days of let's say maybe David Copperfield, Long John Silver or, even, early-Sterling Hayden or Buss Melvin: days when men still gave other men time to prove themselves by their actions and not their bank accounts or appearances.

You see, I'm a hopeless romantic. My only problem is my inability to adjust to the mid-twentieth century. Anyway, there are a few ways to get around these vile border guards. Among them is "pooling" enough money to get a visa into the country. Three or four people put all their money in one pile then take turns going into the various embassies to prove their wealth. Also, some airline tickets can be purchased and then traded back to the company for money. Often times it's not the long hair that matters as much as the other appearance. So I've had a nice pair of slacks made, still have the snappy cowboy shirts that you bought for me, and a little polish might slide me through. Here's hoping! So, I'll see you within two months or two weeks.

In a few days I will send you a copy of the book that I have written on the Tibetan language. Thirty-four pages in all, with a cover designed by a friend and carved by Tibetans onto a wood block. It will be sold here in Kathmandu and it is a sample of what I would like to do for a total of seven languages all in one book, the best buy available to the tourist. This particular one on Tibetan has met with a surprising reaction here in Nepal. It seems that nobody has ever done this before for the Tibetan language. It also seems that many people want to learn the language, so a lot of copies will be sold while I am away in the States. There's not really any money in it though, just a lot of proud feelings (and high hopes for the bigger book).

I'll write or wire as soon as I have made the which-direction-to-go decision – in two weeks or so.

Love, Milan

11

TRADING GEMS AND METAL ACROSS ASIA

Milan wanted to stay in Asia.

That's when I realized I had to make money in Asia by buying and selling things in Asia, and sending things back from Asia to the States. I had met a guy named Dem on three separate occasions. Once in Morocco, once in Nepal, and then on New Year's Eve Thom O'Hair and I were broadcasting live the Winterland show. This guy Dem was there.

He said to me, "Look, I've run into you in three terrific places in the world, and I'm trying to figure out how to make money to stay in places like that. You got any ideas?"

I said, "Yeah, I do. I see all these things in the Himalayas that could be brought back here and sold to Americans. They seem to be very interested in Tibetan religious relics and objects. People are becoming interested in Buddhism and the jewelry, the turquoise and the coral. There are lots of things. But I don't have any money."

Dem, who was a merchant mariner, said, "I'll tell you what. Here's a hundred dollars." And he gave me a hundred dollars right out of his pocket. "I'll go to work on the coal ships in the Great Lakes in the winter and send you all the money I make and you invest it and we'll get a business going."

There was such an openness and an honesty that I had to come up to that level of commitment. I did just that. I went back to Nepal and I bought a bunch of things with the money that he sent. I made a trip back to the States and I sold it all and we made a bundle.

We made enough for me to tell him, "I think you can quit the ships and come and help me collect stuff and then we'll make alternate trips to the States to sell the stuff." That's what we did. We were buying and selling turquoise and Tibetan jewelry. There was turquoise, lots of beautiful coral, amber that the refugees were bringing out of Tibet and selling in the refugee camps.

That began three or four years of wild gem trading. You can't trade gems in Asia without smuggling. That's what it's all about, moving something from a place where it's cheap to a place where it's expensive without giving the government any duty. We did all kinds of things.

Just before Christmas in 1973, Milan sent a long business letter to his sister, who was helping with the trading work in the States. After the details about costs and air freight and customs and sales potential, he added these insights into his life in Nepal.

I gotta tell you something about Dem, – *he wrote* – he's the cream of man's crop. Super soulful, energetic, honest, and the closest thing I ever had to a brother (next to you). It's his money from the coal ships that started all this. It's his energy that keeps it going. Please give him all the help and love that you can during this flurry of business that is about to descend upon your house. Take him in my place for these holiday times and ask Mom to burn a pumpkin pie or a roast for him. I give him a lot of flak about being a hippie, about his trail manners at the table and all of that, but our folks should dig him just the same and I know he'll like them.

I can tell you about the only break that we had during this last week of work madness: Namgyal got married yesterday. Namgyal was the teenage Tibetan who walked into my life in short pants about two years ago. He has worked for me and with me ever since, growing all the while. Yesterday Namgyal, the Tibetan gentleman, was wed to a beautiful Tibetan woman here in our house. He calls me "father" sometimes, but I think it's generally the other way around. I've learned more from watching him bloom than any other single event I can think of. He explained to me that Tibetan weddings are for life (alluding, I guess, to our Western ways, especially mine) and that this day was the most important day of his life. The moment was chosen by a lama, although no lama was present at the ceremony. He spent every last rupee he had on the food and preparations, well over a thousand. Me being the cynical asshole that I can become, I never cry at weddings, except out of boredom. But yesterday got to me.

Namgyal's wife to be arrived with her party early in the morning, her head and neck buried under prayer scarves. There was a simple small carpet with the Tibetan swastika formed of rice on it near the first step into our house. She was met at this carpet by Namgyal's mother, who gave her a bowl of tsampa and a sip of chang. She was bent very low in a bow all the while. I was trying to take photographs, but the overwhelming humility of the bride put me in tears – me and the camera lens. No telling what the photographs will be like.

The bride crossed the threshold and the marriage was complete. That simple.

The rest of the day Namgyal and his wife spent in a small room upstairs. With them was a bride's maid, his mother, and the mother of the bride. Also in the room was an altar with the photo of the Dalai Lama.

During the day a procession of Tibetans came to the house to give their consent to the marriage. Namgyal, his wife, the bride's maid, and the two mothers sat cross-legged in that room for about 12 hours without moving. The procedure was this: people brought prayer scarves, six of them. The first went on the altar, the second to Namgyal, then the bride, the maid, and the mothers. Everyone brought a small envelope with a few rupees for the couple, which was placed on the table before them.

It is now – *Milan wrote* – some 36 hours after the bride's arrival here and the party is in full swing still. After the initial rush of the prayer scarf procession, the food and drink was served. Everyone got smashed and that always means a time to sing and dance and gamble for Tibetans. I could only make it until about midnight, but awoke this morning to find everything looking and happening exactly as it did when we went to bed.

The sharp pop of the dice cups rings out from all the rooms in the house. The guests are all blurry-eyed wrecks, looking like the morning after a group acid trip in an American commune. Nobody slept more than two hours and that was only when they passed out.

I wish you could be here to see and feel it. These words don't do it justice.

Then it was back to business in the letter, details about US Customs duty, and this request:

It's very important that you report to me what happened at Customs each time on each package. Anytime I can figure out a way to hose any government and avoid giving them nickel one, I want to do it. Not to mention saving the bread for ourselves. Tell me all you can: did the post-man deliver it, did you have to go down to the office, what did Mr. Customs man say that might have given you any clue how I could re-label any item to make it cheaper, etc. Ask them all you can about the various things and maybe they'll give you some hints for us.

In Puerto Vallarta Milan fondly remembered the Asian smuggling days.

I went into Burma, way north where they were cutting jade. It was illegal to export jade out of Burma. I taped jade all over my chest. I had virtually a jade suit on and passed through customs and got to Thailand and sold the jade in Thailand. Then I bought gold in Thailand where it was an open market. We smuggled the gold into India where there were government regulations restricting importation of gold. There was also a

At the Taj Mahal

very high premium paid on it during the marriage season, around March. We smuggled the gold into India and one of the things we bought there was the raw material of that stone that you're wearing there.

Milan smuggled the lapis lazuli for my and Sheila's wedding rings for a wedding present, explaining the details in an email to Sheila from Mexico.

The stones for the rings came out of Afghanistan. The raw material came out of Afghanistan but the stone was cut and polished in Jaipur, India. We traded gold for it that we had smuggled into India from Thailand. (I just want you to know that I endow all gemstones with as much adventure as possible for the health, longevity and prosperity of the recipient.)

At the time, he offered marriage advice and more in this letter.

25 June '75

Dear Peter and Sheila,

Nice to return "home" and find your letter. Many surprises enclosed therein, most enjoyable of which was your little poem, a pretty little ditty.

Now what is this about you all "finishing up" with Nevada? Movin' out? I've envied you that little house, such an American (which I am) archetype house and home – room to spread your shit out and work or study or just stare at all your spread-out shit. Doesn't matter, just the walls count. I wish we could get this teleportation number down a little better so we could pull quick switches from time to time. It would expand our horizons greatly.

And "marriage?" Really? What a great idea and what a silly-ass thing to do! I know marriage (know-whadda-mean?). Four times now. The first three marriages were for love and they were miserable failures; this last one was for Airline Discount Tickets, and it's working super fine. We fell in love after the fact and I love it. I must say I enjoyed each wedding. The first took place in a funky black Pentecostal Church on San Pablo near the old Cabale. My ole lady and I were the only o'fays in the room and the band was a rockin' 'n' rollin' and I was happy for at least a half an hour of the ceremony. It went downhill from there.

The second wedding took place up there on your turf. Zella and I roared up to the Courthouse, much to the polite horror of Sweet ole Liz, me wrapped in greasy leathers and Zella as near naked as 1965 would permit; the Harley melted the pavement under it.

The third one was celebrity city. I married a princess masquerading as a poet's widow, everybody who was anybody was there to sing or to film the event, and I was Sweet Sir Galahad soaring to unknown heights, and I remember leaving my room and walking down the hill towards where the ceremony was to take place and midway David Crosby and about six friends walked up to me and said, "Hey, wanna little snort before you go down there?" "No thanks, David, not right now." Then I think I remember David mumbling something like, "Jump 'im," and suddenly six cats (all roadies) bunched around me, my head was pulled back and a shovel full of white powder was super charged into my mind. Ding dong wired from the collar bone up and numb to boot. One of the results of that was that I didn't get laid that night and it was further downhill from there on.

So, there you have it. A quick rundown of some of the sillier moments of my married and married and married life. There are other funnier secrets but my father told me never to put anything on paper that I didn't want everyone to know about – please eat this letter.

Regarding the Lapis Lazuli you requested – I got it. You mentioned a stone about 5 x 7 mm, which is tiny, but I put aside the finest piece we had and we do have the "fine" 'cause I just went half way around the planet to get the best. I also put aside a larger piece for Peter. I will get them to you as soon as I can do it and feel safe about it. The mails ain't safe, but maybe I can find someone flying back there soon who will mail them from within the States to you. Accept the stones as a wedding gift and may they make you laugh every time you think about it, or me, or yourselves. Be patient, OK? I'd like to hand you the stones personally, but I don't see us coming back that way for quite some time. Plans now are to either buy or build a boat large enough to haul cargo and provide a living for us as we goon on the winds.

India? A bit o' hell this time around. The conditions of this journey insured the discomfort in front. We dove into 110 (in the shade, and there was no shade) days/daze, attempting to do combat with Muslim gem merchants who have been waiting out there in the Rajastan desert for about three millennia, sharpening their axes and preparing for our arrival. It shakes one's faith a bit to meet sharpie after burn artist after thief after pickpocket after hustler. In the end we found what we were after, a family we could trust and all the wounds healed quickly. They straightened us and we will make money and so will they and all will prosper. Inshallah!

We were almost touched by the Mayaguez action. One day en route from Indonesia to India we stopped in Singapore and between business binges we snatched a boat and took a harbor cruise. In the harbor was an aircraft carrier, which turned out to be the Coral Sea. The crew was mostly on leave, those few who remained aboard were sort of lazily dabbing paint on this or that. We remarked about how nice it was that the war in South East Asia had come to an end, or at least that our homeland wasn't responsible for such death and destruction anymore.

Three days later we were in India aghast over a newspaper that reminded us that the ole death and destruction was as near as General Ford's phone, that the Coral Sea's planes were dumping all they had on the folks of Cambodia (and, incidentally, that we had a stash of gold bullion in Thailand which we worked very hard for and might not see again). The rest is history. (We did move our stash down to Singapore upon the rebound.) Prediction on Thailand? The locals say, "If the Americans leave Thailand everything will be OK; if not, there will be war." And, "This year will tell, either we go communist this year or never." No telling really. It is clear that the governments of Cambodia, Laos and Vietnam have some internal concerns, but many Thais feel they will eventually look toward Thailand as the next place to continue acting out the lifestyle they have been trained in for the last 30 years, war.

Asia at this point in history reminds me of a jig-saw puzzle that has been turned upside down, all the pieces falling to the floor. All the "leaders" are zooming around to all the other countries making up new deals, trying to get the pieces of the puzzle to fit their own way. Imagine! Mao and Marcos shaking hands. Really, I get the pissed-offs. I see this elite club of "national leaders," some called communist, some capitalist, or whatever, but all the bastards are simply in the BUSINESS of manipulating their own people for their own personal benefit, be it for money or a place in the history books or whatever. Answer? Too idealistic to work, but: expose the hoax of borders and allow mankind to work it out on his own without the help of leaders, the useless.

Such a rave.

'Scuse the incoherence. Remember, between the mind and the hand lies the elbow.

Hope you enjoy the enclosed photos, just a random selection of snaps from our recent run.

Be well, you three, and please give my love to all the folks at home. Do stay in touch and be sure to send your new address should you get one, and I'll continue these tirades.

Love,

Milan

Business, he reminded me while we talked in Mexico, boomed.

Dem went on to Bali and had a lot of these semi-precious stones set, and then either he or I would come back to the States and sell them and we began this mad three- or four-year-long dash of buying, selling, smuggling, moving, trading, all of this metal and stone.

Never caught at any borders?

No, never caught at any borders. Never were caught.

Luck or skill?

We tried to use our brains. There were ways to do it. For example, if you wanted to smuggle something in to Nepal, like gold, you cut a deal with the pilot of the plane so that he would carry your bag in the captain's cabin. When the plane landed you went through customs without your goods and then the captain would come to your house later that night and give you your goods for a fee. Customs didn't search him or he had his guys that he paid off or something like that. We tried to use our brains about it and minimize the risk of getting busted.

How did you get the gold into India during marriage season?

We had these tailors that would who would build suits for us to carry. The gold dealers, the gold shops in Bangkok were cooperative, too. They would pound ingots super thin so that we could wear them in harnesses around our bodies.

These were days before metal detectors and strict airport security.

One time we were flying from India up to Nepal. This wasn't even on a smuggle. The plane left Calcutta and got up over the top of Kathmandu Valley and it was just socked in, all fogged in. There was no visibility and that plane didn't have any landing capability without visual. The captain announced that the plane was going have to return to Calcutta. I noticed the aisle across from us an Indian guy sitting there, who went white-knuckle. I watched him as we landed and I wanted to stay close because I figured he had to smuggle something up to Nepal which, if we went back through customs in India, would cause him a great deal of grief. I stayed right behind him in the customs line and the customs officer, obviously another Indian, told him to open his suitcase and he said, no, he wasn't going do that because the suitcase was never opened since he left India.

The customs officer was on to him and he said, "Open your suitcase."

He said, "No, I don't need to. The plane didn't stop anywhere. We never landed."

The customs officer reached over and, and threw the latches on the suitcase and the suitcase flew open, just whop, flopped open. Inside of it were watch bodies, not the bands, and brassieres. Padded brassieres, which is what made the suitcase fly open.

By the spring of 1974, Milan was writing to Carl Gottlieb that it was time for him to move on, out of Nepal.

It's getting weird here, especially for me. Some drunken renegade immigration officer has begun a campaign of harassment. Wants money and a whiskey he calls "cock-nick," which I assume is Cognac. Instead I give him promises of a partnership in a thriving export business. Maybe we can hold him off until we split here in about three weeks. The bastard knows too much about me and asks too many questions about why I have only Tibetan friends and no Nepali ones, why I like to go to these "restricted areas" and live with these Tibetan barbarians, etc. The answer is obvious to me, but I couldn't tell him. This particular bastard threatened deportation, bloody faces, and blacklisting from Nepal if I didn't cooperate. It's a drag and very depressing after having spent all this time here living so freely.

I did tell all my friends last year that if they wanted to go to Nepal they should go quickly. Most of them moved too slow and now it is too late. You came and went just in time. Nepal is still good for the standard tourist who wants to take a picnicky trek to Jomosom, but anything special or out of the ordinary is now almost out of the question. I will make one more run here in the fall, but a quick one. There are other places.

Bhutan, for example. I met a Bhutanese man while in India in January. He and I have written back and forth several times since then, and he assured me that he can arrange a long visa for me this Fall.

Hooray for new horizons.

Another letter came to the Gottliebs chronicling more adventures.

10 February '74

Dear Carl and Allison;

No telling where this will be mailed from, maybe Nepal, maybe America. I've gotten into the practice lately of taking my important business letters out to the airport, which I stalk until I find someone flying on to America, then I give them the letter, a short story, and a piece of turquoise if they agree to mail it upon arrival in America. Sometimes I put the "hiya" letters, like this one, in the same hands. I know for sure that some of my letters are not getting through when I entrust them to postal facilities.

I was glad to hear that you got your carpet and that you like it. Gonpo and his family were happy, too. Little do they know where it lies now, little do they expect the perversions that might be perpetrated on it at any minute.

The remainder of our trek was successful. Bonnie and I made it to Nyubree, to Tchoo Mik's home, hung out, scored a little treasure, took lots of photographs, crossed the pass, made it down to Palantar and flew back to Kathmandu. Actually, it wasn't quite as uneventful as that. Two days above Arughat Bazaar we met Michael Aris, the tutor to the King and the Royal Family of Bhutan. He was coming down from Nyubree after a partially successful photographic mission. He went up there to photograph all the holy books in the Nyubree Valley. Because of his background and his language he received full cooperation from the main lamas up there, and they opened up all their ancient stash of books to him. He was unable to capture four of the books, though. Michael and his camera could never land in the same monastery as these four books. Too many conflicting letters were sent out to too many helpful lamas and Michael and the books chased each other all over the valley for a solid week.

When we met Michael he related the story and asked if we would try to track the missing books down. Luckily, we were able to do so and the head lama extended full privileges and honors to us, too. I thought I had seen all there was to see in Nyubree the first time I went up there. No way! It was all behind monastery doors which were shut to me until I showed up with a letter from Michael. All the doors were flung open (I'm not completely sure of that). The lamas let me continue photographing long after my assigned mission was completed. I got to shoot their main monasteries, the insides of their private meditation rooms, and the lamas themselves. Unfortunately, I was holding only 8 flashbulbs so I had to stop just when the going got good. Really missed that strobe attachment that Kristine has.

Michael is now living in Burma and he and I are writing back and forth to each other trying to figure out how to get the film to him in some safe way. The books that Michael found in Nyubree were incredible. They were the declarations of descent and power given to the kings and head lamas of Nyubree, they were signed and sealed with the hand print of the FIFTH Dalai Lama. Incredible stuff.

Another innovation and addition to the excitement of this season's trek to Nyubree was a full-out chase by the Nepali Army. Really! There were only two of them, and scruffy looking ones at that, but they were the Army and would have shot us if we hadn't turned back to meet them. It happened just as we were about to cross the pass. We had been in the Valley for about two weeks and we were loaded with treasure.

The Army had an outpost at Sam Do, the last village before the pass (which they didn't have last time). We knew they would be checking our packs before they let us leave the Valley, so we sent Tchoo Mik and a pal named Karma out of the village in the pre-dawn hours. Karma waited a few hours out of the village and Tchoo Mik slipped back in so the Army cats could see him leave with us. Then we made a very loud and obvious exit from the village waving "Anglasie Bye Bye" to the cops. They just waved back and we thought we were free. We moved up the lower reaches of the pass to where Karma was waiting with our stash, then looked back and discovered the Army jamming up the pass after us. Tchoo Mik came through again. We were seven people and Tchoo Mik started shouting orders like a quarterback: "Everybody bunch together tight and head up the pass like we can't see the Army. When we reach that ridge, Karma, you drop the bags behind that rock, then we'll 'see' the Army and turn back." The idea, of course, was to bunch together so the Army couldn't distinguish from that distance exactly how many bags we were carrying. It worked. We dropped the bag off and 'saw' the police and headed back down to meet them. They asked Karma what he was doing up there without a pack and he explained that he was looking for a stray yak – a likely story. They searched everything but our assholes, then they turned back.

We made the pass a little easier for ourselves this year by taking it in two days instead of one. We scored a tent (nomad type) and pitched it just below the snow line on the first day, then zoomed over easily on the second day. You must see the slides from this year. Everything that was covered with snow and snowstorm last year, all that terrain that you couldn't see in the slides, was painfully clear this time. We could see all the way to what we were sure was Mongolia.

Carl, you should soon receive some of that money that I have owed you all this time. Our big Christmas rush was a dud. My partner, Dem, got there too late. But, the stuff still sold, or much of it anyway. The plan is this: Dem departs America on February 28th and he is to bring every penny that we have to our name. Many things have been fronted to stores and this money will come in to my sister. I've already asked her to send you the next $100 that comes in and to repay you in lots of $100 as they come in. Do you remember how much I owe you? I don't. I think it was in the area of $650, then I paid you $100, so maybe it is somewhere around $550. But, honestly, Carl, I don't know for sure, so please tell me if this is incorrect. Again, I'm sorry it took so long. I've put aside the writing and dreaming that I want to do and am devoting all efforts to that ugly endeavor called money. It's working, though, and I'm somewhat sad to say I will be able to pay you back and won't have to borrow any more.

I'll see you in May or June. In the meantime, I'll write and hope you do the same.

Be well,

Milan

Milan's business with Paul Deming continued to grow.

We decided to get professional and mass-market gems to America. In 1975 I moved to Thailand and Dem moved to Bali. Dem would have masters made of Balinese designs and send them up to me, and I built the first silver casting factory in Bangkok. That worked for a while, it was the knock-off version of all of this beautiful hand-made jewelry that we were taking out of Bali; this was the commercial cast version.

The business boomed and Milan was able to pay off debts.

Carl, dear Carl,

Here's the last bit o' bucks I think I owe you.

I just completed a $23,000 sale and I'm turning back flips and trying to write at the same time.

Please acknowledge receipt of these two checks, by postcard or phone call or whatever, so I know you got them. I'm taking off to Nepal in three or four days. The trip will be a quick one, maybe three weeks. The passes are open and the caravans are coming down. I gotta meet them.

Thank you again and again for the long-term loan. I'm liquid (in more ways than one) and shouldn't need such a courtesy again. I'm sorry for the times that you must have thought, "That motherfucker is over there fucking off on rewards of my hard work." I felt it all the way around the planet.

We retire New Year's Day. Wanna come spend a taste of the Spring on a junk in the South Seas? We'd love to have you and Allison aboard.

Be well.

Milan wrote several pieces – fragments of his autobiography – as he traveled the world throughout the Seventies. This recounts his visit to Israel.

I had been living in Nepal for a couple of years and was steeped in the Hindu religion of India and Nepal and the Tantric Buddhism of Tibet. By this time I was speaking Tibetan, Nepali, Spanish, and French. I had discovered that there were many similarities between the most basic words in these languages, like "mama," "madre," "amah," etc. and the idea of a prehistoric language common to all peoples of our planet began to occupy my thoughts. The more I dwelt on this concept the more I became obsessed with the notion that there must have been a religion common to all prehistoric people. Somewhere back there in a time before the current religions began to bend the truth for their own purposes was the shadowy realm of Animism and it must be there that the one real fundamental set of truths existed and I was determined to unearth it. I had a pretty good handle on the two great Eastern religions but I needed to check my data against the three major Western religions.

When the opportunity to travel to Israel presented itself in the form of an airline stewardess who said something like, "If we got married we both could travel all over the world for free," I jumped at it. What the hell, I'd already been married three times and I no longer understood the difference between "marriage" and "affair" or even "date," so I married the chick, bought a copy of The Bible as History and boarded a plane for Israel, the heart of the Judeo-Christian-Islamic experience.

After a quick look around Tel Aviv, which reminded me a lot of El Cerrito for some reason, we snatched a rent-a-wreck and zoomed off into the desert in search of remains of the Israelite Empire from the days of David, the Rock Slinger, and Solomon, the Copper King. We tracked down just about every event in the Old Testament, minus the carcass of Goliath, of course, between Eilat in the south, where some stiff winds in the wadis inadvertently helped Solomon's engineers invent Bessemer smelting, and Jerusalem in the north, where the western wall of his temple miraculously survived centuries of bearded guys with side curls stuffing notes in every crack and attempting to pound them in with their foreheads like a bunch of whacko woodpeckers.

The thing that amazed me most about Israel, though, was the size of the place. All these momentous events in our Judeo-Christian-Islamic history occurred in an area roughly the size of East Oakland (before the landfill). You can stand over the seven levels of Jericho (only one of which was blown down by Joshua, so one wonders who was in the horn section on the other six occasions), look south and see the Dead Sea, look north and see where the Naz bopped across the Sea of Galilee, and look west and see the monastery where He was tempted by Satan. All this action was really just daily life in the "'hood," which got blown way out of proportion, right?

Wrong! Or so I was beginning to believe by the time I got to Jerusalem, which good goyim save until last because that's where their Main Man finally went down to the Romans. Most of the sites involving the Naz in Jerusalem are related to the last act of His play.

I was aware that the locations of all these scenes were identified by Emperor Constantine's mother, Helena, in the 4th century, who, in a psychic frenzy, strolled around Jerusalem arbitrarily decreeing that "this" is the garden where Judas ratted on the Naz, this is the "spot" where the Naz straightened the little cat with the bent frame, "here," "here," and "over there" are the twelve stations of the cross, the Via Dolorosa, which leads to the Church of the Holy Sepulchre where the final events unfolded, but I also realized that so many devout worshippers had visited these sites in the last sixteen centuries and believed that these events had actually occurred in these very places, that the sites were indeed sanctified by the sheer weight of all that trust and belief.

Emperor Constantine built the Church of the Holy Sepulchre to enclose the site where his mother said the Cross had stood, which, fortunately, is just a few feet from the Tomb. As I slowly descended the well-worn steps from street level down into this inner sanctum of Christendom a strange feeling descended over me. Layers of skepticism were rapidly melting off my usually cynical self and by the time I reached the bottom of the stone steps I discovered that I was suddenly a Christian again, a true believer. I looked to my right and there it was: Calgary, where my Lord had died for my lowly sins on that wretched, blessed Cross and directly ahead of me was the holiest of the holy – the Tomb itself! I could barely breathe. I was floating in a cloud of incense. I could barely see. The candles and incense burners on the many altars and shrines of the various Christian sects from all over the planet, which seemed to be flung against the walls by some tremendous centrifugal force emanating from the Tomb itself, were all beginning to ooze together through the mist in my eyes. I was almost deafened by the echo of the shuffling feet of millions of pilgrims who had come here to pray during the past 1,600 years.

I had to do something. I was passing out. I had to move. An inner voice told me to do a "kora," a Buddhist term meaning to circumambulate a holy site, so I slowly, almost painfully, started walking around the carved stone walls of the Tomb in the center of the cathedral. The millions of devotees from the past shuffled along with my every step. As I reached the back wall of the Tomb I saw two darkly robed, hooded monks, probably Coptic. They were seated in the faint light on the stone floor facing one another in what appeared to be quiet meditation with their shoulders and heads pressed against the Tomb itself. I remember thinking about how wonderful these two pilgrims must feel to have travelled so far and to have reached their ultimate goal in life – to be at one with their Lord as they rested on His Tomb, the Holy Sepulchre. This must be religious ecstasy at its highest!

I began to tiptoe past them so as not to disturb their reverie, when suddenly one of the monks spotted me, thrust his arm out of his long sleeve, and reached out to me. In the upturned palm of his hand was a bright shiny little object. He said, "You! Want to buy a cross?"

His words did not compute. I quickly reviewed the facts: I was a devout pilgrim, a representative of millions of true believers who had come before me, and he was a holy man, a near-saint reveling in religious ecstasy.

"What?" I whispered, leaning down until I could clearly see the ornate plastic chromed cross in his hand.

"Cross! Want to buy?" he rephrased for me.

Then the truth of the situation hit me and I started to laugh, I was loud at first, then super loud as true hysterics set in. I sat down on the floor and the millions of pilgrims past sat down with me and they began to roar with laughter, too. Even the monks were laughing and slapping their thighs as we sat knee-to-knee guffawing directly into each other's faces. All together we filled the cathedral with roars of laughter until I thought the arched stone ceiling would shatter and come tumbling down upon us joyful mortals (and immortals).

Inevitably, I could take it no more and fell onto my side gasping for breath and clutching my stomach in agony. When I was able to speak again I thought I would explain to them what I thought was so funny but I realized that deep down they understood and all I could say was, "Thank you! Thank you both! That was wonderful! You have taught me so much!" The millions of pilgrims past had faded and I was about to but, wanting to remain their chump until the very end, I gave each of them an American dollar. I let them keep their chrome crosses for the next true believers who might stumble into the Holy Land.

So, my friend, be on the lookout for upturned palms bearing crosses, crescents, or Stars of David! It is a great opportunity to have the laugh of your life!

This one is about his Tibetan friends.

When most Americans think of Tibetans, the Dalai Lama jumps to mind. He was raised in the Potala, the central palace in Lhasa, to become god-king of Tibet. From the time he was three years of age, his teachers were the wisest philosophers of their land, the most devoted guardians of the Tantric Buddhism. I have tremendous respect for the product of their teachings, the Dalai Lama. If he is not a god, at least he was educated like one. Portions of his final exam were recorded on film by Lowell Thomas. It is a fascinating documentary during which the Dalai Lama displays his knowledge of Tantric Buddhism in an oral exam. Actually, it is more like a debate between one student and the entire academic community of his nation. On a crowded stone courtyard this teenaged god-king-to-be repeatedly pounds his palm with his fist, strides confidently back and forth in front of all of his mentors, demonstrates to them that he has mastered all of their teachings and proceeds to teach them a thing or two of his own.

But Central Tibetans, called "sweet mouths" by Tibetans from the other provinces, not as a derogatory term but out of respect for their formal education and use of the language, are only one of the three main subcultures in Tibet. The other two are the Khampas, the warrior clan of eastern Tibet, and the Drokpas, the nomads of the west.

Literally, "Khampa" means "man from Kham," the eastern province bordering China on the east, and Sikkim and Bhutan on the south. But to most Tibetans, "Khampa" means warrior, brigand, horseman – the equivalent of America's legendary Apache Indian. The Khampas have been called "the Dalai Lama's army" by some, which, if you know anything about the gentle philosophy of His Holiness, seems more than ironic. For centuries, the Khampas fought off the Chinese and repelled all of their invasions until Mao Tse Tung took the reins and, acting on the strategy planned by his predecessor, Chiang Kai-shek, invaded Tibet with massive force. The Khampas, like the American Apaches, were simply overwhelmed by the bluecoats.

During major uprisings against the Chinese in 1950 and 1959 the Khampas formed an organized brigade and escorted the Dalia Lama out of the country to Sikkim and, later, deeper into India, where he is centered today. Since this occurred in the second half of the twentieth century and since it involved armed conflict, one need not look too far into the story to find involvement by the US Central Intelligence Agency.

One Khampa friend told me of travelling in the disguise of a beggar south across Nepal to its border with India, where he and a few score of other Khampas were placed in canvas-covered stake-trucks and transported to an airport somewhere in India. The men were herded from the truck through a canvas tunnel to an airplane with no windows and flown for what he described as two days to another unknown airport. Again they passed through a canvas tunnel into vans that had tape covering the windows.

While in the van on the road, my friend peeled back a corner of the window tape and saw a word which he did not understand but he has never forgotten: it was "Butte" – as in Montana. The Khampas, some still dressed in their beggar disguises, were taken to an undisclosed military base, given new camouflage clothes, and trained in guerrilla warfare for several weeks. Eventually, they parachuted back into Tibet to share their new knowledge with their compatriots. This secret war in Tibet is a little-known story detailed in a little-known, out-of-print book called *Cavaliers of Kham* by Michel Peissel (Heinemann, London, 1972) – captivating reading.

The Tibetans I want you to meet are the Drokpas, the nomads: the "black tent" shepherd/farmer/traders of western Tibet whose lives revolve around the yak. The yak provides milk, yoghurt, butter, cheese, and meat to eat; leather for boots, saddles, and belts; tails for weaving ropes, bags and clothing; horns for tools; and the hides, which make up the black tents. The yaks also transport all these products to market. Drokpas move their animals up and down the Himalayas, depending on the season, and sometimes across the mountain range, depending on the goods they have to trade.

During the warm season the Drokpas accompany their herds as they graze the high Himalayan meadows, and they plant barley and millet crops of their own. During the colder times they move back down to the plains, sometimes visiting the larger towns in Tibet, like Lhasa and Shigatse, where they trade surplus goods for commodities like rice, and other modern essentials such as wristwatches, radios, and cassettes of music from Hindi movies.

The nomad ethic forged on these well-worn trails (in extreme weather conditions) is simple: Take shelter in my tent tonight, Traveler, tomorrow I will need shelter in yours.

For an anthology of travel writing I was gathering and edited, called Perilous Journeys, Milan contributed this account of a trip he and Mocean's mother took to Laos.

The Time: Mid-December, 1974.

The Objective: Enter Laos, visit the Wats of Luang Prabang and stroll the Plain of Jars.

The Problem: Laos is bordering on chaos, soon to be closed to foreigners.

Luang Prabang, the ancient royalist capitol, is in northern Laos at the confluence of the Mekong and Khan rivers. It's a saunterer's Shangri-La with over 30 temple complexes (Wats) bearing exotic handles like Golden City, Buddha's Footprint, Bamboo Forest, Water Dragon, Peace Pagoda, Calling for Rain Buddhas, and Red Chapel of the Reclining Buddha.

There's also the Watermelon Stupa, primitive Animist shrines under age-old Banyan trees, sacred caves containing ancient artifacts and textiles – hill tribe weavings of rare beauty – to tickle anyone's fabric fetish.

The Plain of Jars, a two-day high-mountain road ride away from Luang Prabang, is the site of one of archaeology's most fascinating enigmas. Hundreds of prehistoric stone jars of unknown origin, some weighing over 6 tons and standing almost 10 feet tall, are scattered over several square miles. We have no idea what they were used for: sarcophagi, food storage bins, rice wine fermentation vats? Nobody knows for sure. I've been dreaming of visiting these two places since I became aware of their existence. Time to do so, at least in this life, appears to be running out.

Just a few days ago the government of South Vietnam announced it suffered 3,000 casualties in its loss of six provinces surrounding Saigon. The war rages on but the end is clearly in sight for the South. Next door in Cambodia, the Khmer Rouge horde seems only days away from toppling that government. In Laos, the Pathet Lao has formed a coalition with the Royalist government but it can't last longer than it takes the Royalists to remove their loot. The Pathet Lao, known xenophobes, will probably close the nation to all outsiders.

It's deeply disturbing to us who fancy ourselves as latter-day Sir Richard Burtons (not the actor, the explorer) to know that most of Indochina will soon be forbidden territory. If I want to see Laos, it's now or probably never.

A few days later I fly to Bangkok, the sex, drugs, and rock 'n' roll around the clock, you-want-it-we-got-it, Rest and Recreation capital of Southeast Asia. I clear immigration and customs faster than I can hum "Sympathy for the Devil" and slide into a taxi. The Thai driver wheels out into traffic, looks back and grins.

"You know, Thailand called Land of Smiles?"

"Yeah, I know."

"You know why Thailand called Land of Smiles?"

"I think so."

"Because everybody always smile."

"Okay."

"You know why everybody always smile at you?"

"You tell me."

"Because they wan' you money!"

The stark honesty of his remarks makes us both laugh. Still laughing he says, "You wan' girl?"

"No, thanks."

He looks at me in the rear view mirror.

"You wan' boy?

"No."

"You wan' Thai stick?"

"No, no."

"You wan' opium?"

"Nope."

"You wan' heroin?"

"No, nothing."

He jams the brake pedal to the floor, skids the taxi to a halt on the shoulder, turns to me and yells, "Then why you come Bangkok?"

"Information," I reply.

He stares back, "Where you wan' go?"

I direct him to the Malaysia Hotel, where I hope to find someone recently returned from Laos. In the lobby I meet a young Dutch man and his girlfriend. They describe the Laos new Coalition police patrols on the streets of Vientiane as "two Royalist guys dressed like South American generals walking by the side of two Pathet Lao guys who look like Viet Cong."

The girl tells me the Lao currency, the Kip, is crashing. Gold is better than dollars up there now. People are "jumping," she says, I should hurry because "something happens now." If I get in trouble, they advise, I should hide in an opium den; it's safer than the hotels.

I cab it to Patpong Road. At the Playboy Club, a hangout catering to US servicemen and Arab businessmen, a doorman presents a laminated, mimeographed menu of the sex show: See Pussy Shoot Ping Pong Ball, Pussy Cut Banana Half, and, my favorite of these Olympian feats, Pussy Write Your Name!

Inside I find an American ex-airman and trade him beer for information and opinion: the US withdrew its troops last June and halted its 10-year bombing campaign consisting of over half a million sorties dropping over 2 million tons of bomb and losing over a thousand pilots. This is supposed to be a secret, he laughs. Even now, with only scuttlebutt to rely on, he reckons Laos is the most bombed nation in human history. He knows Luang Prabang was never hit but doesn't know what's left, if anything, on the Plain of Jars.

All the next day I wonder if it's wise to enter Laos and conclude that it isn't but decide to go for it anyway. It's not 100 percent safe, but neither is Life. Besides, adventure involves risk and risk implies threat; but the threat seems manageable. If it gets too nasty, I'm sure I can bail to safety one way or another.

En route to the train station I stop on Yaowarat Road, Bangkok's ethnic Chinese-run Gold Street, and trade a few hundred dollars for two one-ounce gold ingots stamped with the smelter's mark and .999. Once aboard the train, I close the curtain on my sleeping compartment, strip to my shorts, tuck the ingots, my wallet, and passport into a money belt, and secure it around my waist. I fold my khaki trousers and a few t-shirts into a pillowcase, lay my head on it, let the rails rock me to sleep, and dream of a dream coming true.

Next morning I cross the Mekong in a dugout canoe and clamber up the riverbank to Vientiane. In Laos at last! Instantly, I see what the Dutch kids meant by "people are jumping."

Laotians and foreigners alike appear to be moving about five frames per second faster than normal. There are no colorful sarong-clad, denim-shirted Laotians chewing betel nut in the shade of Banyan trees. Everyone is in motion, on their way to somewhere else. Most are carrying some sort of parcel and appear deeply absorbed in their own thoughts. Many cast furtive sideways glances. But this frantic pace is only in the eye of the beholder; maybe I've got still-sickness after the all-night train ride. If so, eating a juicy red-gold papaya could calm the belly and the mind.

The morning market is an open-air affair with faded fabrics stretched over bamboo frames to shade the vendors stretched out along the roadside. The stalls behind them, three-quarters of the space, are empty. Pickings are meager, but I find a small papaya and offer a Thai Baht note in return. The seller, a towel-turbaned older hill tribe woman, flashes me the first smile I've seen in Laos thus far. She tucks the note into her sarong, then pulls a wicker basket down from above, reaches in, grabs a fistful of small Lao kip bills, and hands me the whole wad. Baffled, I attempt to make some sense of this transaction by organizing the brightly colored bills by denomination. The other women vendors start to laugh and make "go-away" signs with their hands. I start to question but the women join in a cacophony of Laotian, Thai and French to tell me, "It's only paper anymore. Don't bother. Go. Go."

Late that afternoon I find a backpacker who has just returned from up country. He informs me that kip is still the currency of choice outside Vientiane and gives me directions to a moneychanger/gold dealer who, rumor has it, offers the best exchange rate. Fifteen people crowd around the small barred window protecting the moneychanger. As I jockey for position I watch a Coalition police squad finishing their dinner in a restaurant nearby: two Royalists, two Pathet Lao – the first Pathet Lao I've seen.

The difference between the two factions is striking. The Royalist patrolmen are indeed dressed like Panamanian army generals on parade: tightly tailored uniforms sprinkled with brass insignia and campaign ribbons topped off with saddle-shaped patent leather-visored hats with a swath of "scrambled-eggs" embroidered above. Their US-supplied M-16 rifles are six feet away, leaning in a corner. The remains of a chicken feast litters their side of the table; an empty whiskey bottle rests in an ice bucket. They're drunk, the only ones in the restaurant laughing at their own jokes.

In contrast, two sober Pathet Lao soldiers sit upright, alert, in well-worn over-size cast-off Russian uniforms. No medals, no insignia; only handmade leather cartridge pouches with deer antler latches accessorize their attire. Their beat-up Russian AK-47 rifles rest in their laps as they finish a mean meal of rice and tea. It's clear to me which side is determined to win this particular war.

The young man between the moneychanger and me is Canadian. I assume this from the replica of his nation's flag sewed to his backpack. I try to buy the flag from him. Not-a-chance-in-hell, he replies, smiling and looking me directly in the eye. He's afraid he might be mistaken for an American.

By the time I reach the window and get a quote on my ounce of gold, it is the equivalent of three dollars higher than when I first got in line. I'm tempted to go to the back of the crowd or return the next day to take advantage of the kip's free-fall, but opt instead to focus on traveling north as quickly as possible. I sense I've arrived in Laos just in time to witness it crash down around me. Time to move.

Transportation north is not easy to arrange. The ticket agent at the bus station has discarded his schedule and sells spots on whatever vehicle shows up. He doesn't know exactly when the next departure for Luang Prabang will be. I hang around for a couple hours with no luck then take a taxi to the north edge of the city. The driver refuses to take me any farther, but suggests I try to wave something down here on the road.

It's winter now, dry season. A hazy sun in a cloudless sky bakes the red earth. Fine ochre dust is everywhere. All I taste, smell, and feel is dust. I fancy I even hear the dust as it settles on my skin, dissolves in sweat, and colors me khaki.

Eventually I get a standing-room-only ride in the back of a stake truck with 20 Laotians, but it lasts only a few hours to Phon Hong. From here I get a bus; but this time it's lying-room-only, atop a stack of rice sacks at the back of the bus.

Another bus, two mini-vans, 200 miles, and two days later, I reach Luang Prabang and check into a cheap hotel. It's a wooden, two-story French colonial residence now divided into a dozen or so crib-size rooms.

Hotel guests congregate on the porch, and I hear nothing but bad news. A middle-aged Canadian man describes the Plain of Jars as a bomb-cratered junkyard littered with war debris. Land mines and undetonated ordinance, such as cluster bombs, wait to explode under unsuspecting feet. That evening a long-haired Frenchman and his girlfriend check in. They're visibly upset. Pathet Lao stopped their bus from Vientiane at an improvised roadblock, treated them roughly, searched their backpacks, and nearly confiscated their passports. They were told repeatedly that foreigners were no longer welcome in Laos.

Next day, I stroll from Wat to Wat hoping the tranquility will dispel my growing anxiety. It doesn't. I can't get into the groove and the temples feel like postcards held at arm's length. I came all this way, but don't feel like I'm here.

That night another French couple arrives at the hotel with another tale of trouble on the road from Vientiane. They witnessed two young Americans pulled from a truck by what they thought were Pathet Lao and marched at gunpoint into the jungle. Other guests joke half-heartedly about escape routes. From the summit of Phu Si, 300 feet above the city, I look down on golden temple roofs glittering in the morning light, but the view brings little joy. I make every attempt to enjoy the Pak Ou caves but I can't shake the feeling I'm experiencing one of Fate's nasty little ironies: I'm here in Shangri-La and wish I weren't. I watch the sunset over the Mekong and vow to forget about the Plain of Jars and leave Laos if things get worse.

I return to the hotel and it gets worse. All the guests are packing. The Canadian man tells me two Australians have been pulled off a bus and shot dead at roadside. None of the guests can confirm this rumor as anything but a rumor. One thing we all agree on is that it's safer to leave than stay. The Australians were shot on the same road I had travelled up from Vientiane, so I opt for an escape by river. I take a trishaw to a pier on the Mekong River. It's dusk and most of the boats are moored and empty. The few boatmen who remain are sullen and unresponsive to my Thai, French, and English requests for transport. Finally, I connect in pigeon-English with a Thai national named Lek. He's going north to Ban Huay Sai (directly across the river from Chiang Kong, Thailand) with a load of empty rice sacks but, emphatically, "No!" he's not at all interested in having a "farang" in his boat because part of his trip is through Pathet Lao territory. American dollars, Lao kip, and Thai baht do not move him. Only my last gold ingot turns him around but he refuses travel at night. We arrange to rendezvous at 6 in the morning at a bamboo grove upstream. No one must know I am with him. He recommends I spend the night in an opium den and gives directions to the closest.

As a sort of rent on my space in the den, I pay for two pans of opium – enough for eight pipes. I like opium but I'm feeling like I need my wits more than a vacation tonight, so I decline the pipe when it comes around.

Before dawn the next morning, I climb into Lek's sampan, a low slung six-plank eighteen-foot double-ended hull with a long-tail motor mounted on the transom. Lek is a bit of a clown and makes a game of our passing from Royalist territory into Pathet Lao and back again. On Royalist stretches of the river he asks me to sit upright.   "You up. You up. You farang. You farang!"

In PL territory he covers me with rice sacks and says, "You down. You down. You rice. You rice!"

Nonetheless, the boat ride is lovely. Undulating limestone cliffs and craggy mountains alternate with jungle, forest, paddy, and fishing villages. It's comforting to be on the move, even in potentially dangerous areas.

At dusk on the second day we round a bend and I see low buildings lining the Thai side of the river; its dock is crowded with 40 or so sampans like ours. I look back at Lek. He nods, grinning. Chiang Kong, Thailand – we made it!

But we don't make it. Lek refuses to land on the Thai side for fear of losing his cargo and boat to Thai customs officials. I'll have to take a ferry or another sampan from the Lao village of Ban Huay Sai. I ask Lek if this village is Pathet Lao or Royalist.

"No Pathet Lao," he says.

I dangle my hand in the water and reflect on my week in Laos. Has it been one long close call like it seems, or have I let my imagination invent nonexistent danger? I'll never know, I guess. It's been fascinating, a story to tell and, though I'm glad I came to Laos, I look forward to the relative safety of Thailand, just a few minutes away now.

But it's not a few minutes away.

We dock in Ban Huay Sai. After talking to another boatmen, Lek reports that the ferry has already made its last run for the day. Most of the other sampans are empty and the few boatmen still at the water's edge refuse to cross over to Chiang Kong.

Why? It's Movie Night!

Movie Night? What the fuck's that now?

Once a month, Lek explains, a Land Rover comes to this village, its driver bolts a 16-mm projector to its roof, and beams a movie onto the white-washed outside wall of a local restaurant. It will start as soon as it gets dark. Lek stands before me embarrassed as I shout that he promised to get me to Thailand and he's not getting the gold until I get there. No problem, he says, tomorrow morning, first light, he will take me across in his cousin's boat because, "Tonight nothing to do, go movie, sleep."

Resigned to another night in Laos, I follow him through the one-lane village. Houses and shops on either side are single-storied combinations of wood plank, bamboo pole, thatch, cement, and metal sheet. Lek's cousin lives and works in a bamboo-walled lean-to with a corrugated metal roof. His name is Yai. He fixes motors. When we arrive he's fixing a pipe, delicately packing its bowl with a tiny donut of opium. Lek and I sit cross-legged on the lumpy linoleum-over-dirt floor. Yai lies next to his lamp, his head resting on a small pillow atop a low coffee tin. Lek motions me to the spot on the opposite side of Yai's lamp; it has its own pillow and tin.

What the hell, I'm out of danger, imagined and real; there's no Pathet Lao in the village, only a movie to watch and a night to kill. Yai swings the pipe around to me, places the ivory mouthpiece so close to my lips all I have to do is pucker, suck, and hold the smoke. Museum   quality   pipe: dark patina on the rosewood shank, ivory end pieces, a chased silver base holding a jade bowl. I take a second lungful. This one does the job. I roll aside to make room for Lek as the Goddess of Serenity wraps her warm, loving arms around me and gently rocks me away to somewhere mellow and safe. A jazz tune wafts through this space, a soft piano and acoustic bass behind the lyrics:

Better than elephants dancing,
Better than clowns on parade,
Better than peanuts and popcorn,
Better than pink lemonade,
Better than rides on the midway,
Better than seals blowing horns,
Better than men shot from cannons,
Better than fresh ears of corn,
Better than anything except being in love.

Lek's voice intrudes, "We go movie now Chaws Bon Son."

He makes a gun of his forefinger and thumb and shoots a couple rounds across the room.

"Hey, I'm fine right here."

"Yai close shop. Go movie."

"Okay, Lek."

Lek, Yai, and I stroll back up the lane expecting to see Charles Bronson punching, stabbing or shooting some cowboys or crooks. Instead, I am treated to a wonderfully surreal scene: about 200 colorfully attired hill tribe folk and villagers sitting silently staring at a blank white wall. Everyone from miles around is here, tightly packed into a small group, most anaesthetized like us, relaxed, ready to be entertained. We ease ourselves down among them, not knowing we are about to be captured.

Suddenly three trucks roar down upon us from the north. The first vehicle races around us and screeches to a halt on our right side, the second brakes to a spot behind us, and the third slides in to our left. We are blinded by headlights and lost in a cloud of dust but one thing is clear: the entire movie audience is boxed in. The only way out is through the whitewashed wall but no one tries that. Through the dust we see fifty fatigue-clad Asian men and boys standing in the camouflaged trucks; most point their automatic rifles directly down at us, the few clutching grenade launchers aim them skyward. One of the soldiers in the first truck hoists a bullhorn and speaks to us in Lao and Thai.

He cautions us to "Stay down, keep quiet."

We sit motionless, barely breathing. Our captors sway in slow motion as their rifle barrels sweep back and forth across us.

A seeming eternity ensues. I am afraid for our lives, yes, but also mystified. There is comfort in the journalist's perspective, to analyze the participants without admitting I am one.

Are these people to be executed?

Why?

And by whom?

These soldiers wear generic uniforms with no sign of origin or rank. Where are these men from? Clearly, they are not Royalist Lao troops, nor Thai, Pathet Lao, Viet Cong, Khmer Rouge, South Vietnamese, Chinese, or Russian.

So, who then?

Finally, the man with the bullhorn, clearly in command, turns to confer with the troops in his truck. What follows is a pre-planned deployment: all his men jump down from the last truck to arrive; six men remain guarding us and a dozen walk south down the village's only lane. They station themselves about 20 yards apart stretching their line to the end of the village. The truck drives down the same direction and parks sideways, blocking the road. The scene repeats itself with the second vehicle, this time on the lane leading north. The leader dispatches half the men from the third truck to the west, between the river and us and the other half to the east, between the jungle and us.

The leader hops back aboard the last truck. He speaks through his bullhorn with the confidence of a man in control. I nudge Lek for a translation. He ignores me and listens intently. People start to clasp their hands on top of their heads and slowly rise to their feet. Lek and Yai do so also.

I look to Lek; he murmurs, "Okay, okay up."

I join my hands behind my head and get to my feet. Shit! I wish I were shorter. I stand head and shoulders above the audience. My bright white elbows pierce the night and shine like beacons above the sea of coal black hair. I feel like a freak and an easy target.

"Okay, okay" Lek whispers, "Yai house, okay, okay."

The audience starts to disperse. People shuffle slowly north and south along the lane under the watchful eyes of the soldiers. No one gets past the trucks blocking the ends of the lane; those who try are turned back and forced into houses or shops.

As Lek, Yai, and I pass the soldiers, I get a better look at them and their weapons. They carry battle-worn American M-16s and M-79s, Russian AK-47s, and a few older pieces I don't recognize. What's striking is the age of the troops themselves – none are within the usual military span of 18 to 35. They're all older than 50 or younger than 15, and a few look like they're about ten.

We reach Yai's garage, Lek motions me to the floor. He joins me near the lamp as Yai turns on every light he owns. Yai and Lek launch into a long, urgent, hushed conversation in Lao at the end of which Yai begins to load his opium pipe.

Lek turns to me. "Meo," he says.

"Meo? What Meo?"

"Meo Hmong take factory."

"What factory?"

"Heroin."

Suddenly, all the pieces fall into place, the puzzle solved. It looks like this: the American military command wants to fight fire with fire, to pit its own "friendly" paramilitary guerrilla units against the guerrilla tactics of the Viet Cong and Pathet Lao. However, the Geneva Accords banned funding for such an army. The Central Intelligence Agency steps in, recruits experienced paramilitary bands like the Meo in the Golden Triangle, trains them and facilitates their self-funding as follows.

Air America, the CIA airline, transports laboratory equipment and chemicals to the Meo, the Meo refine opium into heroin, and the CIA flies the heroin out to market. The Meo spend some of their huge profits buying American-made weapons to fight the Viet Cong and Pathet Lao. Everyone on the American side should be happy, right?

Wrong!

The scheme has disastrous results. The market for this heroin turns out to be the American GI on "R and R" in Saigon, Bangkok and Manila. Certain unscrupulous individuals in the US military transport massive quantities of heroin back to the States using methods as macabre as stuffing body bags. The long-term effects on millions of Asian youths will be devastating.

The Meo, first fooled by the French, now tools of the Americans, have lost thousands of young men to this war in Laos, and their forces have been reduced to old men and young boys. They know the Pathet Lao will soon take the country, and the new regime will not tolerate opium consumption, let alone heroin processing. The Meo have come to this village to pack up one of these factories and remove it to Burma.

The arrival of the Land Rover with the movie projector may or may not have been part of this Meo unit's plan but it served to get all the villagers to the same place at the same time.

We remain on the floor for two and a half days. On the morning of the third day, Lek peeks out the window then throws open the door. The Meo are gone.

So am I!

Lek takes me to the Thai side of the Mekong in Yai's boat. I thank him and hand him the gold.

"You know, Thailand called Land Of Smiles," I say to him.

"Yeah," he smiles. "Merry Christmas."

It is indeed the 25th of December 1974.

Both Bob Dorough and Al Jarreau recorded the jazz tune mentioned above. When I asked lyricist Bill Loughborough for permission to reprint his words he not only agreed, he penned this new verse:

Better than Laos incursions,

Better than opium dreams,

Better than tunnels through jungles,

Better than wading in streams.
Better than napalm or "orange,"
Better than Saigon delights,
Better than clean black pajamas,
Better than one-sided fights.
Better than taking friendly fire,
Or chanting "LBJ's a liar,"
Better than anything except being in love.

Another Asian experience Milan shared with Mocean's mother was an encounter with pirates. Mocean is the hero.

My partner Paul Deming and I had made good money selling Thai gold chains that year, and we had bought a teak-hulled 40-foot Thai river barge, installed a centerboard, fitted the interior for cruising, and had her junk-rigged to be a fast-sailing Chinese junk. We named her "Lorcha."

In March we left Bangkok, en route to Bali. With us were my wife Bonnie, our infant, and Barry, an Aussie friend helping crew.

At that time, three years after the fall of Saigon, it was common knowledge that fishermen-turned-pirates had attacked boat people attempting to cross the corridor between South Vietnam and Malaysia. Their pattern was to rape the women, rob the men, kill everyone, strip everything possible from the vessels, then scuttle them.

We sailed down the west coast of Cambodia, hugging the coast until we drew a few warning pot shots across our bow from small-arms fire, then headed across the Gulf to the Thai island of Ko Samui, giving a wide berth to the corridor area. After a stopover, we left to follow the Thai and Malaysian coastline down to Singapore.

Late one windless morning, we were on diesel power under fair skies and nearly flat seas, when Barry, who was alone on watch topside, yelled that four big boats were heading for us.

Within minutes they were within hailing distance – four Thai fishing trawlers: big, wooden-hulled 80-footers, three stories tall. On the decks of each there appeared to be about a dozen crew, crouched and working on their nets, or pretending. One of the boats was obviously in command and it pulled up close alongside to port until the leader at the railing stood no more than ten feet from me. The remaining boats moved quickly, one pulling in front of us, another to starboard, and the last just astern. The throbbing of their diesel engines was incredibly loud. The leader made a hand signal to his crew and they dropped their nets and appeared to be in a stand-by-to-board mode. By then Paul had joined Barry and me on deck.

The leader yelled to me in Thai, "Have you any cigarettes?"

I responded in Thai, "No, I don't smoke."

"You got any whiskey?" he asked.

I answered, "I don't drink."

"You got any money?" he yelled.

I was bare-chested and wearing a sarong, and I pointed around the boat and answered, "Naw, we're just going to Singapore to try to find some jobs."

He said, "Okay, now we'll see what you do have."

About six guys from his boat approached the rail, as did another four from the boat to starboard, all preparing to board us. Then, at that exact moment, my wife Bonnie appeared on deck, wearing a sarong and carrying in her arms my little bald-headed one-year-old son. She had come up in complete innocence, having no idea of any danger. She showed no fear.

I watched the captain as he looked, not at Bonnie, but at the child. As soon as he saw him, something in his eyes changed. He looked at me, and then back at the baby. Then he gave a flick of his wrist and instantly his boat peeled off, as did the one to starboard, followed by the remaining two boats. They were gone, just like that.

We were stunned. During the encounter we knew we were about to die. I felt the captain had no qualms about taking the three of us men out, and Bonnie too. But crossing that line and taking out a baby was not something he was prepared to do.

In the aftermath I felt like a total failure as captain, because I had brought my family and two friends into this mess without a way out. Earlier we had all discussed ways to arm the Lorcha to repel boarders, but then I realized, with four boats and 48 of those fuckers putting us in a box canyon, there ain't no way out. It was clear by the amazing precision those pirates demonstrated that they had played this thing out many times before.

To this day I know that my son appearing at that precise moment saved our lives.

In this letter home, Milan urged his family to come share the adventures.

4 February '74

Dear Mom and Dad,

Enclosed is another letter that I wrote about six weeks ago. I just discovered it and flushed with embarrassment. It's been a long time since you've heard from me and I apologize. As the other letter said, business has got my brains completely occupied. It has indeed paid off, though, and we are on our way to a strong import business organization. To hell with business, for a few minutes anyway, at least long enough to write you.

We are back from India and we had a great time, an educational time as well. I was able to take several rolls of photographs of the people and the Dalai Lama himself. (Someday I'll do something with all these photos.) The Dalai Lama has an interesting history. He's a young man of 39, but an old and wise man in his appearance and training. He was 25 years old when Tibet fell to the Chinese and he had the heavy responsibility of guiding his people through a very tragic time. The Tibetans believe that he is an incarnation of Chenresig, the God of Mercy. He may or may not be – I don't question other people's beliefs. But, here's the important thing – he was educated and trained from the time he was 5 years old as though he was that God. He was given the most extensive education that anyone ever received, probably. He shows it, too. I'm not a "guru follower," I've never come home and said, "Hey Mom, hey, Pop, we all should follow this man." I'm basically a very skeptical and sometimes cynical man. But the few minutes I spent in this particular man's presence gave me some insight into the potential that exists in all men – with training, any man can be anything, any man can do whatever he wants, he can get and receive whatever he wants from life. It's hard to put it into words. Suffice it to say that I saw a man that I very much admire and respect and it is a result of training and education and, above all, CONCENTRATION. That experience has given me my second wind, so to speak. ALL IT TAKES TO BE OR TO DO WHATEVER ONE WANTS IS CONCENTRATION. The best part of it is that it is free, too.

To get a little more down to Earth, we received a very nice card and note from the sweetest of all hearts, Auntie Gena. Enclosed were three photos of your Christmas Day and one old photo (taken in 1937) of Pop Melvin and Uncle Rel. It really thrilled me, and Bonnie, too. One Christmas photo showed you two sitting on the couch at home, another showed the chair that I should have been sitting in on that morning, and the last one showed my pal and partner, Dem, receiving the shirt that you gave him. The photos brought me much closer to you all. The other photo, the old one, showed Grandpa and my great-uncle (a man I never really knew) standing in front of Va's Crocket house – and a really fine picture it is, too. Such a proud man, that Uncle Rel. So strong-looking, yet so relaxed. I value that photo very, very much and I packed it all around our little village and forced everyone to look at it. I make one request of you two – please write me something about him. Tell me anything you can remember; write me a short biography. Where was he born, did he marry, did he have any children, what was his profession, what was he like, when and where did he die? Really, I'd like to know anything you can remember. I'm completely fascinated.

Pop, you mentioned a boat in your letter. I really hope you buy it. I'll be back in June and that ought to be a good time for a little fishing together somewhere in those Sacramento sloughs, right? A ride around the Bay wouldn't be bad, either. A 25-footer, though? We could damn near cross the Pacific in that. I'd be willing to try if you would. I know you don't trust planes very much, so that may be the only way that I can get you over here. We have plans for a boat, too. A bigger one and a stranger one, but a boat, nonetheless. I've spoken to you about this, I think. We want a Chinese junk – a broad-beam, slow-moving, but sturdy ship – something in the 75-foot range. She'll have a shallow keel (which is good for moving in close to all those South Pacific Islands), but they are so wide that you can't roll them over. I'll tell you more about it as we get closer to actually buying one. The salt in me blood, ole mate.

Mom, you mentioned that you were thinking about coming over here and that really thrills me. You would like it very much, I think. Janelle wrote me a letter in which she said that you were worried about whether I would have "room and time" to spend with you. Now, that's the silliest thing I ever heard. Did you have time and room for me in your womb? Of course you did and of course I do. Please, please come. Bonnie and I would love it. We have a nice house now, complete with hot water (which is damn rare around these parts) and I would love to show you around this country. We could fly up into the mountains for about $15.00 and play in the lakes in a dug-out canoe. We could take long walks in the morning sun, we could surround ourselves with the Tibetan children at the nursery, we could just sit on the porch and talk (which we haven't done enough of). I have two men working for me that do all the cooking, laundry, and errands, so you wouldn't have to think about dirty dishes. Come play!

Both of you should come; it's cheaper than you think. After all, I owe you about 20 years of excellent care. I wish you would give me a chance to return some of it.

You both wrote that the rings arrived and that you like them. I'm very glad. Both are special pieces. Dad's matches mine and Mom's matches Bonnie's. Wear them in good health. We were both proud to send them.

Our life is still very hectic. I still spend most of my time at this type-writer trying to direct our sales operation in America. Dem is doing a fine job for us, but he requires much thought and encouragement and connec-tions that I must provide. The nursery requires most of Bonnie's time and she does it without complaint. She's a strong woman (and I love her very much). Sometimes we look at each other and agree that we are working too hard at our business and at our nursery, so we decide to take mark a certain day as our holiday. Then that day, that holiday, comes and we just settle into a little relaxation when someone shows up with their daughter who has a terrible skin disease and has had it for the past three years. So, we spend most of our "holidays" at the hospital with someone else's child. It must be done, though. Both of us are a bit run down, but still healthy and very happy, so we can report that life is still good to us. Bonnie and I are very much in love and there is no sign of any dark clouds on the horizon...

In Puerto Vallarta, Milan asked me to find Dem and engage him to share a story of their adventures together. We met in a shopping center in Contra Costa County, California, where Dem sets up shop during the Christmas holidays, selling artifacts from Bali. He grew dreamy with memories as he talked about their cruises on the ship they bought with the earnings from their trading.

The first time when we headed out into the ocean, where you couldn't see land, we were going to go all night long across the Gulf of Siam. We were in Thailand. We bought the junk Lorcha in Thailand. I remember Milan questioning, "Are you sure you know where we're going to end up?"

I had marine training. He had none.

I told him, "Yeah, we'll stay on this course. We'll basically go that way. You figure the wind is blowing this way a little, so we've got to adjust the course a little that way."

We didn't sleep a wink that night. We both sat up all night long on the helm, steering this boat that had just a hand tiller, no wheel on it. We crossed over into the Cambodian waters from Thailand to Cambodia. Now you'd be arrested by military gunships in a second. But back then you could actually do that and get away with it.

It was early morning and still no sight of land. We were tired from being up all night long. All of sudden, the fishing reels started to spin and whine. Milan was on the back of the boat fighting the biggest fish he had ever hooked in his life. There was a beautiful sunrise. There we were on our little yacht, with this big fish. It took us an hour to get it in. Mocean's mother took a picture of us. I'm standing there naked. Milan has his Thai sarong fishermen's pants on. That's what I think of when I think of the Lorcha.

We sailed around the entire Malay Peninsula.

Probably the most incredible story is when we got hit by a sumatra. It looked like an eye on the horizon, these heavy duty winds from Sumatra that come shooting across the Straits of Malacca. We were out there and we looked out and saw this black eyebrow – just like Milan's eyebrows – coming at us. These things are going 80 miles an hour. We were trying get the sails down before they ripped, trying to get things tied down. This wind hit us so hard. Anything that wasn't tied down just got blown off the deck. The sea turned white all around us. We had never seen the sea so churned up and foamy. It hit us so hard for about 15 minutes and then it was gone. It was like being in a hurricane for 15 minutes. That's how fast they move over. The wind was blowing so hard we couldn't talk. You tried to open your mouth to talk and the wind going in your mouth drowned out your voice. I was afraid the whole boat was going to be blown over and churned into the water like being in a juicer. It hit us right at sunset, this big black eye. All the heat in Sumatra builds up during the day. Then all of a sudden it bubbles up and takes off, the winds created by the hot air rising and the cold air rushing to replace it. That was probably the most frightened we ever were on the boat.

We sailed the Lorcha all the way down to southern Thailand. We did all the islands. We sailed it down to Bali, the two of us, our first trip to Bali on a boat, sailing between Java and Madura in the night. We had no radar. One guy stood on the bow yelling, "Turn right! We're going right into a boat!" Screaming all night long, running over fishermen's nets.

Then we saw Bali, the volcano up through the mist. We couldn't see the rest of the island, just the tip of the volcano. We'd made it from Thailand all the way down to Singapore and down to Bali.

Mocean took his first steps on that boat, stood up for the first time.

Milan often noted the unusual locales where he found himself experiencing history, as in this memory of Nixon.

Often I hear the question, "Where were you, what were you doing when you heard that JFK was assassinated?"

I don't remember, but I do remember the exact second I heard about Nixon resigning.

It was August 10th, not the 9th, because I was in Nepal. Chan and I were lodging with half a dozen other foreigners in a tavern of sorts along the Nepal-Tibet border. The place was a holy Hindu purification site complete with 108 brass naga head water spouts that poured forth freezing water from the snows above. Chan and I had just finished our breakfast, burned up a bowl of super potent hashish, shed our clothes, descended down into the stone bathing area, when a guy who had hung behind in his sleeping bag in the tavern threw open the shutters and screamed, "Nixon just quit!"

He heard it on a shortwave broadcast of the BBC. Chan and I looked at one another in total disbelief; then, along with five other trekkers, broke into a wilder than Shiva himself version of his dance of destruction as we passed under and bathed ourselves in each of the 108 naga heads. I rubbed dead skin off my body with a rock and remember thinking of it as Tricky Dick himself. When we calmed down, a good hour later, I never felt cleaner or freer in my life.

Fuck that decomposed motherfucker in the heart forever!

In a letter to a friend in the States, Milan listed what he missed and wanted.

Things that come to mind immediately are things like a jeweler's drill, dried apricots, the Grateful Dead on cassette, rawhide boot laces, an apple pie made by my mother, a slap on the back and a "How you doin', son?" from my father, a look at my sister, a bottle of Scotch, a San Francisco Chronicle, Shaklee's Protein Powder (if the Japanese haven't bought up all the soy beans in America), some ballpoint pens, some big posters of cows and horses, ten million multiple vitamin capsules, and your own sweet self.

Milan kept close track of what was occurring in the States, relating it to the cultures where he was currently living, in his letters home, such as this one.

This just in from David Crosby:

Lorena Bobbitt is driving on the Interstate right after she did the deed. She looks down on the seat, spots the evidence, picks it up, then flips it out the car window. Splat! It slams against the window of a semi-truck traveling at high speed in the opposite direction. The trucker turns to his ole lady and says, "Ma, did you see the dick on that bug?"

Yes, penis cutting is a tried and true Thai custom. I searched for but cannot find a collection of articles from the *Bangkok Post* which I clipped almost twenty years ago. I wanted to send you copies, but alas! What's left of memory will have to do.

The series of clippings started out rather simple. Knowing that his wife was aware of his extramarital affairs, Arnon Chulalongkorn wore eight pair of underwear to bed. He awoke in the middle of the night to find his wife slashing at his private parts with a razor. Arnon was able to escape before any damage was done to his manhood.

The second one broke the ice. Somkid Supanayon awoke in the middle of the night to discover that his wife had amputated his male member and thrown it out into the lily pond beside their house.

The third gave more details. Karoon Krittiyanon awoke in the middle of the night to discover that his wife had severed his male member and thrown it out into the lily pond. A duck was seen disappearing with the amputated organ.

The fourth edged toward the surreal. Sommai Pranonakorn awoke in the middle of the night to discover that his wife had cut off his male organ with a razor and thrown it out into the lily pond. A duck was seen disappearing with the male member. Suddenly realizing the implications of her actions, Sommai's wife, Noy, immediately rushed her husband to a hospital with a sausage, asking doctors to sew it on her husband until she could find the duck.

The last one brought it all full circle. Kaseem Phitalonan awoke in the middle of the night to discover that his wife had amputated his male member and thrown it out into the pond beside their house. A duck disappeared with the organ. Repenting her action, she rushed her husband to a nearby military hospital where, coincidentally, a surgeon, Lt. Col. Sononakorn, was performing a sex change operation down the hall from her husband. When told of Mrs. Phitalonan's need, the surgeon rushed to Kaseem's bedside, sewed the unwanted male organ on to him, and called a press conference to announce the world's first successful penis transplant!

How's a writer to beat that?

A Thailand travelogue was included in that letter.

One weekend in Thailand I decided to go to Pattaya by myself. I always took the bus down there because at the time there was only a narrow two-lane road and the A.C. bus was the largest vehicle I could find to transport my body there and back. I always sat in one of the aisle seats in the very center of the bus. Clearly it was the safest commercially available seat in the country. The trip back was uneventful until we got within half a mile of Sukhumvit Road at which time I happened to look up from my book just in time to see an on-coming cement truck pull out to pass and slam directly into the front of our bus, knocking it into a roll and off the road into a swamp, where it came to rest on its side.

When my head cleared somewhat I kicked up at the window, popping it out, then climbed up onto the side of the bus. As I began to help other passengers out of the bus I noticed their looks of horror. Though I felt no pain, I was sure that some damage had been done to my face as it impacted the metal ashtray mounted on the back of the seat in front of mine. But shock can be a wonderful thing. Once I was sure that everyone who was going to get out of that bus was already out (and there were at least a dozen people in the front three or four rows who never would get out of that bus except in baggies) I started looking for my suitcase. The baggage compartment had flown open and people's stuff was scattered all over this muddy bog. I remember high-stepping in slow motion, sorting through the debris, collecting my gear and even taking time to inventory all my belongings to make sure I had everything.

By this time a huge crowd had gathered along the road. I ambled up the bank with my suitcase, calmly refused medical attention, walked across the road as if nothing were amiss, and climbed into the back seat of a taxi. Though the driver had seen the entire scene, I explained to him that I had been in a horrible accident in which many people had lost their lives and that I wanted to avoid any possibility of another mishap so I requested in perfect Thai that he drive very slowly. I thanked him in advance and told him that there would be a handsome reward in it for him.

The driver nodded his head in complete understanding, jammed his foot to the floor, and, within a hundred yards, slammed into the back of another vehicle.

By now I was becoming inured to this and simply thanked the driver, got out of the taxi, strode forward of the entangled vehicles, and got into another taxi. The driver turned to ask my destination and reacted in proper horror to my bloody face. I explained to him that I had been in two accidents within a hundred yards and that I would pay him double the normal fare to drive no faster than 10 miles per hour. He agreed and I gave him my address. He turned forward and immediately stuffed his foot to the floor. I, in turn, slid over behind him and placed both my hands so tightly around his neck that it cut off most of his air. I told him to slow the vehicle to 10 miles per hour, which he did instantly. I released my grip somewhat, but kept both hands around his neck for the entire trip across Bangkok from the south to the north.

As soon as I was out of his taxi he sped away, but not before I thrust the entire contents of my pocket – probably two or three thousand baht – in through his window onto the back seat. Either the driver found it later and was very happy, or the next passenger found it and was even happier. I couldn't give a fuck. I was home safely.

Speaking of vehicles, have you noticed the mud flaps on the Thai trucks yet? Many of them used to sport images of movie stars like Chaws Bon-son and Clint Eastwood, which hipped me to the fact that getting one's face on a truck's mud flap far outweighs all other forms of notoriety. The Oscar is only recognition by one's peers within the industry, the Nobel prizes are awarded by Scandinavian intellectuals, but Thai truck mud flaps mean worldwide fame. My favorite one of all of them is the one that shows a Thai man dashing across his yard with his wife in close pursuit. She has a firm grasp on the back of his shirt with one hand and in the other she wields a meat cleaver. Completing the picture is crowd of ducks hoping, no doubt, to get that soon to be detached penis before Lt. Col. Dr. Sononakorn sews it back on to someone.

12

BACK TO AMERICA: THE FARM IN WOLF CREEK

Back in the States from Asia, Milan found a photograph of his great-grand-father deep in an Oregon archive. Milan bought a farm in Wolf Creek, near his namesake's homestead. There he cultivated vegetables and more stories.

What follows started out to be a simple notice of change of address, then quickly tumbled into a full-blown newsletter, statement of major change of lifestyle for my family and me, and an invitation to you for my Fiftieth Birthday Party. Not to worry if you cannot make it all the way through this document, just tear off the letterhead and keep it with you in case you find yourself stranded in Southern Oregon and need a place to sleep.

Georgeanne and I sold our house and holdings in California and parlayed the profits into a place in Oregon. We "bought the farm," as they say, an historic 64-acre farm named Red Gate Ranch. It is located two miles east of Wolf Creek (population 200) on Coyote Creek Road. It has a small four-bedroom house that was built in 1889 and a huge barn that looks like it was built a century before that. Twenty-seven acres are in irrigated pasture that has seen everything grow on it from alfalfa to strawberries to elephant garlic, and the 37 acres across the year-round creek (Coyote Creek) are a forested box canyon called Kennedy Gulch. The property is surrounded by BLM land so it will never be developed, and we can plan on seeing trees growing on it forever.

One of the interesting features is the water rights that came with the deed. Since the house was the first settlement in the canyon, it has the oldest water rights to the entire creek, including the watershed. This means that we control the use of the water of Coyote Creek, and Georgeanne and I can add the titles of "Water Master and Water Maiden of Coyote Creek" to our resumes. In order to prove that real control of the water flow actually came with the property we went upstream to a mining operation and asked them to stop using water and shut down their operation temporarily. They did, with a "Yes, sir, Mr. Melvin," so we bought the place.

As you may know, Oregonians are notorious for hating Californians who come up to their state. But, in my case, it is more like a homecoming than an invasion. I display my settler-ancestors credentials proudly. As I dug into the local historical museum in our nearby county seat, I found photos of my great-grandparents (also Milan Morrell Melvin) with my grandfather as a child. It seems that my namesake was a bit of a wacko himself. He came from back East by wagon train as a young man and settled a major hunk of territory in the triangle formed by the junction of the Umpqua and Smith Rivers.

He became a state senator in the early legislature but he is remembered most for championing the rather bizarre journey of "The Swan." This boat was a rear-wheel paddle steamer. The crazy old bastard, Melvin, decided that central Oregon needed an inland port so he and scores of workers paddled, pulled, and pushed "The Swan" up the Umpqua River from its mouth at Reedsport, all the way up to Roseburg (the California equivalent of this would be like driving a steamer from San Francisco to Placerville far up on the slopes of the Sierra). The odd thing is that they made it. The iron eyebolts which they embedded in the bedrock of the river to pull the steamer up over the rapids still exist.

I was in a cafe along the Umpqua River near one of the tougher points of the ascent of "The Swan," and a waitress approached me and asked if I had any sisters in the area.

I told her, "No."

She then bent down close to my ear and in soft conspiratorial tones whispered, "Mister, you got two exact female doubles that live right close by here."

I take that to mean that either I have some distant relatives along this stretch of the Umpqua or old man Melvin was driving something more than eyebolts into bedrock in that neighborhood.

The state of Oregon is a strange mixture of liberal idealists and redneck reactionaries. In pockets like Ashland there is the world-renowned Shakespeare Festival and during the theater season the town is packed with actors dressed in New York threads who screw their eyes tight against the morning sun as they rush towards the nearest cup of cappuccino; in Eugene a wonderful university community thrives, and in Portland a strong environmentalist movement seems to have a voice. But the remainder of the state is much like it was during Civil War, when Oregon was the only western state to support the Confederacy.

Trucks abound with bumper stickers that read, "Save a Logger. Eat an Owl!"

In the local bars, hand-scrawled signs are pinned to the back-bar such as this one: "It's a dog-eat-dog world and I'm wearing bone meal under-wear." It's signed by "Peggy."

Snatches of conversations are overheard in grocery stores along the lines of this one:

Child: "Daddy, I want some candy."

Father: "You gotta eat yer dinner."

Child: "I want candy for after dinner."

Father: "We'll shoot that duck when it flies over."

At a local jam session, my son-in-law, Chip (Georgeanne's daughter's husband), was being eyed by a rather large woman who had been singing earlier in the evening. She wore a cowboy outfit with a huge oval belt buckle and was missing a few teeth in front. Near the end of the evening she managed to back Chip into a corner. She placed her two hands firmly on his shoulders and gave them a good squeeze. Then she did the same to his waist, finally reached down, carefully and expertly weighed his testicles and said, "Twenty-eight, huh?"

Chip stammered, "No, twenty-seven, and married with kids." Large Woman replied, "That don't matter, honey; so am I. Wanna know what I do for a living? I break buckin' broncos. You ever ride one?"

"No."

"Ya wanna ride one tonight?"

Anyway, we are loving the idea of having a farm in rural Oregon. We have already moved all of our personal possessions and our business's merchandise up to Red Gate Ranch. Mocean is enrolled in North Valley High (which has half the number of students per classroom as his school in Santa Barbara) and I enjoyed kissing the lovely but lame little town of Santa Barbara good-bye on Valentine's Day, to be exact.

Now, I know you are asking yourself, "What are the Melvins going to do for a living?"

First of all, Georgeanne will continue to operate Flamingo Designs and its line of women's apparel, Fit-To-Be-Tied, from Oregon because she is a talented designer and the line sells well across America, even in this near-depression economy. But I am getting out of the rag trade. It's been a nice ride but it ain't me.

Secondly, we are going to grow everything we can on our new land, except marijuana, which is way too obvious and, since the inception of the RICO laws, much too dangerous. They confiscate everything you got. We plan to bring our fallow fields back to life with "green manure" crops like legumes, sweet peas, and wild flowers that will fill the valley floor with a riot of color while replenishing the top soil. We also plan to start year-round production of organic vegetables like that stuff in your salads, and hardwood nursery plants like that stuff in your yards and on your shelves. And, finally, we want to try an alternate protein source like fresh water crayfish – we have 5 huge ponds on the property and the water is too cold to swim in, so why not turn the ponds into food factories?

Farming quickly became hunting.

I was too excited about planting an organic garden and putting in an orchard on this newly acquired piece of paradise to consider that the animals who have used this portion of the planet as a main thoroughfare since time began would be interested in eating fresh fruit and vegetables that magically appeared in their path. Thus began The Deer Wars of 1992.

I didn't drive up here in my rented nouveau prairie schooner (a Ryder truck with a car trailer in tow) until the middle of February and I didn't begin construction of the redwood raised boxes until April. Bare-root tree planting season was nearing an end and it all had to be done quickly, so I hired three guys and we attacked the building and planting of the garden boxes and the construction of a deer fence all at once. We worked 14- and 16-hour days and progress was dramatic, but not quick enough. Even though we had a six-foot fence in place within days of planting the semi-dwarf trees we noticed that leaves were rapidly disappearing from the Gravenstein apple trees. All that was left in trade for these juicy tidbits were tiny turds, definitely deer.

I was sleeping out in the orchard hoping that the combination of this six-foot-high fence and my presence would deter them. I set my alarm to wake me every hour so I could shine my flashlight around the orchard and scare off any would-be nibblers. After all, there must be a humane way of dealing with such things. (Often I would awake in the middle of a dream featuring herds of camel-sized deer with huge tongues that issued forth from giant smirks to lick my face as they stared down, mocking me). But they kept coming and the trees were getting more naked by the night. The locals said that my fence wasn't high enough to keep these pole-vaulting ruminants out of the orchard. They suggested repellents, everything from blood/bone meal to cougar piss, many of which I tried, but I drew the line at the women's-panty-hose-stuffed-with-human-hair-from-the-barber-shop idea.

"Human hair never loses its smell," they said.

Too kinky, I thought. Besides, after working 16-hour days for weeks without a break, I was the strongest smelling human thing alive anyway and I was sleeping right there between the apples and the strawberries.

So I opted for the high-tech approach. I bought a solar-powered electric fencing kit and strung this hot wire along the full length of the perimeter, which now stretched to over 700 feet, enclosing almost a full acre. The wire, if touched by a deer, would deliver a 4,000-volt jolt, not enough to fry them but enough to make the statement that this part of the planet was no longer theirs. They would learn and they would stop coming. I went to sleep that night under the stars convinced that I had dealt with this in the most humane way possible under the circumstances and that I would finally get a full night's sleep.

About one in the morning I dreamt that I heard a soft nibbling sound alternating with the pawing of a hoof on the earth.

I remember thinking, "Isn't this funny. Deer could never get in here now and yet if one did this is exactly how it would sound."

I opened one eye and sure as shit there she stood, a big fat doe standing right next to me munching away at the leaves. The next thing I remember is that I had her cornered at the far end of the orchard. I stood there naked except for the flashlight in one hand and the .357 magnum in the other.

I was shouting, "I'm going to kill Bambi's mother and then I'm going to fucking eat her raw!"

I had only two bullets in the gun, and I missed with both. I felt like throwing the empty gun at the doe, like they do in bad movies, but instead, like they do in even worse movies, I charged her. The sleep deprivation, my fear for the lives of our baby trees, and the construction fatigue all obviously had gotten to me, because people who try this sort of thing on a cornered deer usually get their brains kicked in. I have no idea what I intended to do to her other than drag her down with my long claws, bite into her jugular vein with my sharp fangs, and hold her there with my brute strength until she died. Fortunately for both of us she turned and bolted right through my brand new chicken-wire fence as if it were made of old lace.

So the next morning, after I told the guys what happened and after they finished rolling around in the dirt laughing, we decided that we would forget about this "deer" fence shit and build a goddamn "giraffe" fence. To make a long story short we pulled up every other fence post, replaced it with a ten-foot post, spanned the gap with a 2 x 4 top rail, re-installed the hot wire on top of that, and then stretched wire fence from top to bottom. No deer have come back inside the garden/orchard since. Bambi's mother is safe from me and we are safe from her and her kid.

The move to the farm led to interaction with the locals.

I purchased that wooden crate full of motorcycle parts from a guy who said that the various mounds of metal would become three complete Harley Davidsons. (Actually, they became two Harleys, one of which was a 1941 shaft-driven military flat head that was designed to fight Rommel in the deserts of North Africa, and one an Indian.)

I hated mechanic-ing, especially the part about stuffing a full sized-human hand into the space of a thimble then withdrawing it with engine oil covering the bloodied knuckles. I don't know why I humped those Hogs for more than three decades except to "feed the rat" within me. I always lived in terror of that pocket of gravel laying in ambush just around the next curve and hundreds of nights I jerked myself awake just as I plowed into the side of that same 18-wheeler-that-came-from-nowhere.

"Worry Is Prayer, Worry Is Prayer," I kept telling myself. If you worry about it enough, it won't happen. But the nightmares continued until I got rid of my Harley, climbed up on a John Deere tractor, offed all my "Live to Ride" T-shirts, and replaced them with hats that read "Rides Like a Deere."

After much of two decades as a youth in East Oakland, then a decade as a marijuana-crazed media maven, then a decade as an American adventurer in Asia, and then a decade as an entrepreneur dabbling in everything from television production to jewelry and even the rag trade, I am farming. Tilling the fucking soil!

Here I am jacking around the fields knowing as much about farming as could be carved on the head of a pin by a spastic stone cutter. If it is true that ontogeny recapitulates phylogeny then I have progressed to the agricultural knowledge that mankind must have begun with in Mesopotamia 10,000 years ago. I crawl around the fields on hands and knees extracting stones from the dust.

Luckily, I found a mentor in the person of Roy-Neil Millis, "Farmer Roy" he's called 'round these parts. He is a cankerous old fart who has been farming every day of his life for almost 80 years, just the type I needed and I had been trying to get next to him since I moved up here. One day he was selling eggs out of his pickup as I passed by with the post-hole digging auger attached to the back of my tractor.

Roy signaled me over and asked, "How much you want to dig me 40 holes in easy dirt without no rocks?"

My break, at last!

I replied, "I'll dig you all the holes you want for the rest of your life for one dozen eggs and some advice on how to farm."

He squinted his eyes, stared at me for what seemed like a month then finally said, "I'll give you two dozen eggs. How's that?" It was a good deal for both of us and, as it turned out, I could not have even turned over these fields that have laid fallow for a decade without his help. He brought over his 65 horsepower Farm-All tractor, the hood of which seems as long as the deck of an aircraft carrier when you're in the driver's seat. At Roy-Neil's suggestion I hired a younger man with strong kidneys to drag that giant double-bottom plow back and forth across these rut-ridden fields.

After the plowing I fell into a pattern of rising at dawn, discing and harrowing the fields; I now know where the term "a harrowing experience" comes from – it is that feeling which you get while riding an undersized tractor up, over and back down between oversized furrows without a kidney belt. It's much like sailing a Chinese junk in gale force winds abeam of a series of tsunamis while Mike Tyson pummels your organs. But before I could plant my seeds I had to irrigate and before I could do that I had to remove the rocks and rubble that had accumulated during the winter in the reservoir in the creek where the irrigation foot valve should go.

I tackled that job with the loan of a dredge from "Texaco Frank." Since this is gold country, I thought I might as well run the material through a sluice box to see if there were any nuggets or flakes of gold to be found, just in case the fortune that has always lived just around the corner in my life might have been waiting here for me all this time. Each morning after the harrowing experience, I would don a pair of nipple-high waders or a wet-suit, fire up the dredge/pump, leap into the creek, sneak up on the 20-foot-long four inch diameter hose and wrestle this angry, writhing boa monster until my shoulders gave out. Then I would crawl up the back steps and into the kitchen, fall over onto my side and wait for Georgeanne to pour some gruel into that hole in my face just south of the nose. Often, mild hypothermia had set in and I felt frozen right down to my bone marrow, so bed was the only option. By the end of the dredging I did accumulate a little "color," as the precious metal is called by those in the know, but the illusive fortune remains around some other corner.

It all worked and, as I write now, I can look out the window and see the oats and Austrian peas (which restore nitrogen to this neglected soil) carpeting the acreage from one end of Red Gate Ranch to the other. This farm is finally on the mend.

But, of course, to become a real farmer, one must join The Grange.

Before moving up here all I knew about The Grange was that many rural towns had Grange Halls in which old people met for bingo games and potlucks. A few months after our move here, a neighbor suggested we join The Grange in order to take advantage of lower insurance rates. At about that same time my teenage son came home from his history class with an assignment on The Grange. These subtle one-two combos often lead to dancing instructions from God, so we took the next step and began to investigate. The more we discovered the deeper we were drawn into this secretive organization.

The Grange was formed two years after the end of the Civil War. It was founded by farm women for social purposes and quickly became the political voice of rural America but not before a life-and-death struggle with the railroads. Literally life and death. Long before they drove that golden spike, which symbolized the completion of a transcontinental railway system, the railroad barons realized they had the farmer by his corn silks. If the farmer wished to transport his crop any farther than he could reach in a day's buckboard ride, he had to get it on the rails.

The railroad bosses reasoned, "Why transport the farmer's goods for him at all? Why not charge so much to carry the crops that the farmer will simply sell us his harvest dirt cheap right there at the depot?"

The farmers rose in revolt and spoke through The Grange. Something like: Robbery! Usury! Monopoly! In response, the robber barons sent Pinkertons, accompanied by gangs of burly tracklayers, to destroy this movement. Grange members and the farm family itself were a target of the best organized muscle outside of the US Army. The Grange scurried underground. It developed a super-secretive system of membership by recommendation, elaborate initiations during which the applicants demonstrated their knowledge of agriculture, constantly changing passwords, obscure hand signals, and sentinels to insure that trusted members only attended the meetings. Once organized, Grange members came back out of their barns with a fury and they whipped the railroads. The Grange busted the monopoly.

At its peak, one-third of all Americans belonged to The Grange. It affected fundamental changes that reverberate today, like mail delivery to rural areas and the right of rural residents to receive electricity from their local utility company.

So, to bring all this back to the present, though I am over fifty (and have received a gift membership to the American Association of Retired People from that smart-ass former roommate of mine, Carl Gottlieb), I remain a sucker for revolutionary rhetoric. The thought of joining an organization that has a history of speaking up for the little guy, of wielding tremendous political clout, and even mauling a few monopolies, I found too seductive to resist. (Besides, a 40 percent drop in my auto insurance rate feels better than pissing on an electric fence, right?) We joined.

One Saturday last fall, thirty of us candidates for membership gather in the headquarters of the county Grange. During this initiation ceremony we swore our secrecy about the event but I can describe it here in general terms without discussing the forbidden. The ritual itself is at once Christian and Pagan, religious and secular, patriotic and revolutionary, militaristic and humanitarian, and cabalistic and community-oriented. That is: similar to the Masonic order upon which it was based.

The opening ceremony reflects the paranoia of the past. Officers secure the perimeters against the railroad thugs. Outer gates close. Inner gates seal. Guardians take their places. Every member in the room whispers the secret password to an officer who reports it to another officer who reports it to the Worthy Master. We candidates remain seated, puzzled.

As you might expect, the Pledge of Allegiance follows. I have a conflict here. Having lived in America during the Sixties and in Asia throughout the Seventies, I remain enraged with my government for what it does to the people of other countries with my damn tax money. When it's right to make a statement about my feelings, like at sports events in large stadiums, I usually turn my back to the flag, and when it doesn't feel right, in tight circumstances like these, where folks will feel confronted, I play along. I place my hand over my heart and repeat my own version:

I pledge allegiance to the flag
Of the Transportation Department's road crew,
And to the Interstate on which it stands,
One highway,
Open sky,
An escape route to freedom for all.

What the hell, it begins and ends the same way as the official one and in the middle it's mumble anyway.

Members sing. Something about Jesus' feet. Then they invoke the spirits of Flora (pagan goddess of flowers), Ceres (goddess of grain), and Pomona (goddess of what? freeways?). Next we receive a history lesson from the Worthy Master about the railroads, the need for secrecy, the works. Finally, the official initiation ceremony begins. Officers select certain candidates to enact life on the farm during all four seasons. Four candidates are blindfolded and led around the room several times to depict the darkness of Winter. They remove their blindfolds for Spring and parade around the room several more times, stopping at the Chaplain's station to pray, at the Lecturer's station to learn, at the goddesses station to be blessed, and at the guardian's station to be reminded of the need for secrecy. Two hours pass in monotony. All the Candidates wonder if the 40 percent drop in car insurance is really worth it. A few eye the door, seemingly ready to bolt, but resist, unsure that if they are captured they will be imprisoned in some kind of Grange hell.

In the middle of this process, we retire to folding tables in the next room for snacks. Norwegian-style snacks. Tuna on white bread. Vanilla frosted white cake.

Midway through our colorless meal, they capture Georgeanne and me and another couple, a biker and his ole lady, to represent Summer and Fall. Back in the main room, officers march us around several times as we mime the sewing of seeds and later the harvesting of the grain. Only two sounds interrupt the death-like solemnity: the soft shuffle of our feet against the linoleum and the ever-increasing hum in my ears which, in my Days of Psychedelia, always signaled the gradual slip into insanity.

I feel an impish spirit creep out of my right ear, slide down my neck, scurry across my shoulder and down my arm to occupy the scythe in my hand. The scythe slowly begins to shadow sword-fight. Encouraged by the titters of the Candidates and the reddening faces of the Officers, the scythe makes a few passes at the more than ample buttock of the officer ahead of it. Candidate hysterics now.

Okay, we got our laugh. Time to get the genie back into the bottle before he takes control. But, he reasons, like most genies, that he spends too little time uncorked and there is so much important work to do. He refuses the bottle, perhaps forever. The spirit in the scythe now works his way back up the arm to adorn the upper body in a puffy-sleeved, billowing-lace-at-the-neck shirt, and then moves down to clothe the legs in tight leotards. The imp within then fills that suit with the energy of a buccaneer. Errol Flynn, to be specific, as he singlehandedly races from port to starboard and then back again to battle scores of scallywags (who are masquerading as Grange Officers and Candidates) on the pitching deck of Blackbeard's galleon. I seem unable to help myself and neither can a friend who appears to be piddling on her folding chair as the Worthy Master reasserts his authority and orders the Fall season brought to a premature close. In the Winter of his discontent, the genie accepts the cork.

Nonetheless, the Officers accept us as members in the fourth degree (each season is a degree) with full privileges to get cheaper car insurance and to attend monthly meetings at our local Grange Hall if we choose.

We do attend the next local meeting. Maybe the theater of meeting with others who share secret code words and hand signals draws us, maybe the thought of joining an organization which might throw its weight behind the movement to protect our environment from the real pirates inspires us, or maybe the fantasy of decriminalizing marijuana with the help of The Grange tickles us. We don't know, but we go.

We partake of some of the local herb in the car en route and then enter the Hall grinning. What we see is right out of the past. Except for the six of us newly initiated members, the youngest people in the room are in their late seventies. Pre-Depression era folk dressed in farmer drag. Bib overalls and plaid shirts on the men, women in plaid dresses, probably from the same bolt of fabric. Straw hats hang on the rack.

I say to the Gatekeeper, "You all look like something out of the nine-teenth century".

"We are," he replies, and means it.

The meeting is also out of the 19th Century. Everyone is checked for the password. We do the Pledge, sing the song "Work till the Day is Done," and settle down to the evening's business. The Steward asks if everyone is warm enough. Receiving only tepid responses, he throws enough logs onto the fire to make it overwhelmingly hot within minutes. The aptly named Agriculture Officer, Rose, reports that the year's work is finished and that we should place all our gardening tools into buckets of motor-oil soaked sand to prevent rust. Yearly elections are held and we discover that we newcomers are included in the power structure. Chuck has been chosen as Lecturer, Pat became the goddess Flora, and Georgeanne the goddess Pomona. Dan, Ginny and I compose the entire Executive Committee. Goddesses and Executives! What could be better?

Without realizing it, we of the Psychedelic Era had begun our gradual takeover of our local Grange from our 19th Century brethren. During the months of meetings that followed we brought a dozen other New Age Neighbors into the fold, mainly with the cheap car insurance angle. Some of the new members do not understand the theater of the Grange and do not attend regularly. They consider the meetings boring – maybe because alcohol is forbidden – and do not share our fascination.

Last summer I felt somewhat the same. The thrill was gone. But, for some reason, I allowed myself to be selected as a delegate to the State Grange Convention, which sets the legislative policy for the entire state of Oregon. Influences national Grange policy and thereby affects a powerful lobby in Washington DC, which speaks for much of rural America. I agreed to attend the week-long convention, hoping to find a faction of folks from my own era who would voice environmental concerns to our national lobbyists.

I have never been more wrong in my life!

I took a seat at the top of the bleachers in this high school gym convention hall so I could read last year's legislative policy and size up the situation without being obvious. I was stunned to read that the Grange advocates clear-cutting of old-growth forest, promotes the use of nuclear power, endorses pesticides and herbicides, and does not object to the use of any chemical additives to our food. In other words, the Grange favors anything that provides a quick profit for the farm and timber industry in the short run. And, oh yeah, forget the future! We'll all be dead by then!

As I scanned my 300 fellow delegates on the floor below I could not pick out one person who I thought might ever have voted anything other than Republican unless it was for the John Birch Society slate. Ninety-nine percent white haired men and blue-haired women, but not a face of color in the lot. It was the largest group of old people I've ever seen outside a rest home. As I listened to their speeches, laced with snide denunciations of "that environmentalist cult," and watched their skits in which they ridiculed the spotted owl, I couldn't help but wish them gone. Bless their reactionary little hearts, I know they are the parents and grandparents of some wonderful loving families, but may they all experience comfortable and swift deaths. Their politics along with them.

I got one, too. One of the Executive Committee, Mort Somebody, cacked on the second day. During the prayer offered for him, all I could think was, "Fuck him. One less Republican!"

So now fucking what? Eighteen of us scions of the Sixties have joined one of the most conservative organizations in the nation and we each support their lobbying in DC to the tune of fifteen bucks a year. And for what, cheap car insurance, a few secret hand signals and a little theater?

Shit!

I had to make a choice right then and there. Either get out or get in deeper and work back out from the belly of the monster. Maybe create one helluva headache for the beast, maybe even constipate it occasionally.

I opted for the latter. At the convention I endured the initiation ritual for the fifth and the sixth degrees, which allows me to go to next year's national convention. At last month's meeting of our local Grange I was elected Master of our lodge. I made sure of this by packing the hall and rigging the vote. I've got some chaos to create and I'm in a hurry.

Recently, at the Oregon Country Fair (an annual gathering of psychedelic cowboys and cowgirls), I shared a joint with another long-hair and told him how strange it felt for a former campus radical and Sixties druggie to have become a member of a radical-right group like the Grange.

"Funny you should mention it," he replied, "I just joined the Elks."

My mind immediately leapt to all those thousands of near-empty Masonic, Odd Fellow, Moose, etc. lodge halls across America waiting for the Space Rangers to come fill them and turn their politics around. As a result, my motto for the Nineties is: Join something and mess with it. Recycle the power!

As a postscript I must add that the process has already begun. At my first meeting as Master in December, I started a short speech about The Grange's need to become as relevant to the contemporary rural community as it had been in the past. I asked folks to think about local issues that might also be of importance to all rural residents.

One lady in her seventies jumped up and said, "I'll tell ya one. Toxic waste incineration right down the road."

In the stunned silence that followed her comment one could hear chins around the room dropping onto our stations (desks).

"What?" we said, almost in unison.

The lady proceeded to detail several months of frustrating work against the passage of a pending Rural Land Development Code. She had discovered a phrase in the "permitted" portion of the proposed code that read simply, "soil remediation." She could not find the word "remediation" in any dictionary so she continued to inquire until she recognized the word as a euphemism for "incineration." By this point her nosing around had introduced her to a few other folks with a great deal of information on how toxic waste incineration is big business. She shared information on the Eastern Seaboard, where unused ore smelting operations are being converted to toxic waste incinerators, and the rural South where massive facilities were being constructed in poor, unorganized, predominantly black counties. She told us of a huge new incinerator built in Kettleman, California, an area populated mainly by migrant workers from Mexico.

What most irked her about the Kettleman site is that toxic waste (everything from hospital burn bags to gasoline additive soaked soil from dead service stations) is trucked to Kettleman from all over the state. The fallout from its incineration (emissions that include dioxin, furans, benzene, and a host of other methy-tri-tetra-chloro-nightmares) spreads across the fields of vegetables in which the migrants work and, since southern Oregon imports most of its vegetables from California during the winter, we damn well might be eating some of it in the potluck planned for later that evening.   Another member expressed concern about our county, and specifically our region of the county, appearing to be an ideal site for construction of a toxic waste incinerator. We are close to the I-5 corridor and a major rail line; politically we are as unorganized as a neighborhood can get and the incineration industry's pitch to "provide jobs" for this economically starved area might find support among the many unemployed timber workers.

Before we adjourned, the lady gave us her sources and contacts. A few of us vowed to learn more about the proposed Rural Land Development Code, specifically, and toxic waste incineration in general.

There has been no turning back since.

We brought the results of our research back to the next Grange meeting in January, laid it out to the members, and a resolution was composed and passed unanimously. We (1) asked the County Commissioners to impose a ban on the importation of toxic waste into our county for the purpose of "remediation," (2) asked that no permits be granted to build any permanent incinerators, (3) asked that all toxic waste generated within our county be dealt with on-site in a state-of-the-art manner, and (4) demanded that none of the above be changeable without a vote of the people of our county.

We of the Sunny Valley Grange took this resolution to the Pomona (countywide) Grange and it too voted unanimously to endorse it and send it on to the County Commissioners. With this resolution in hand, we approached every single organization in the Sunny Valley/Wolf Creek area that had a name (the Volunteer Fire Department, the Merchant's Association, the Civic Association, the Citizen's Advisory Committee, and an environmental group, King Mountain Advocates). We asked each group to co-endorse the Grange resolution and to send it along with a cover letter to the Commissioners, the newspapers, and select members of the state government. All the groups did so.

The replies came simultaneously from the Commissioners through both public and private channels. Publicly they said that "soil remediation" had been dropped altogether out of the proposed Code and no one need concern themselves with it any longer. Privately they said that the Master of the Sunny Valley Grange (yours truly) was a liar and they were furious with him for causing unnecessary public disturbances.

Awright! Got their attention. Now to get their obedience, like good elected officials are supposed to give.

The organizations listed above, by now known among themselves as the Little Six, called a meeting last week with the most irate Commissioner. He verified that "soil remediation" had been dropped and backed it up in writing.

But when asked, "If an issue as potentially dangerous to public health as toxic waste incineration could be so easily dropped from the Code, could it not be just as easily added back in?" he had to agree that, yes, the three Commissioners could put it back in at any time. He swore they would not.

Right, Nixon was not a crook and Reagan knew nothing about Iran-Contra.

So next step is a county ordinance that enacts the four points above as law. And if it's a good enough ordinance, maybe it will fly for the entire state of Oregon. The Grange has lobbyists in Salem. Of course, once past the state level we would not be doing ourselves justice if we did not at least take a shot at the federal stage. After all, the Grange has paid lobbyists in DC, too.

On the other hand, I may just move back to Asia and open an employment agency to provide American domestic help to Asian families. After all, the 21st Century will belong to the Asians and America will become its Third World supplier of cheap labor so I might as well get a jump on the crowd.

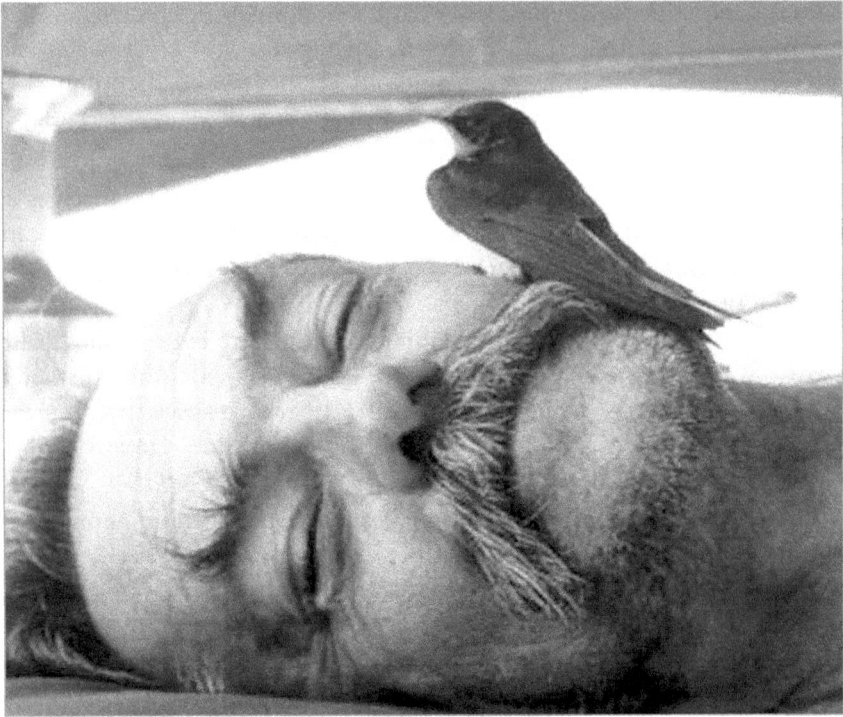

13

Diving into Mexico

Instead, Milan moved to Mexico with the same sense of wonder that he enjoyed in Europe, Africa, Asia and Oregon. He reported:

Went to the dentist, he repaired my teeth and didn't charge me. Same day, went to an attorney and he had portraits of Nelson Mandela and César Chávez on the wall. I must be in Mexico!

And this:

Mexico can sneak up on you, and usually does. Just about the time I get pissed at endemic mañana-ism, the endless cajoling of locals to get something done (or undone), or begin to lose my cool all over some poor bureaucrat in an office whose fault it wasn't for putting our home address (which has no mail delivery) as our mailing address for the phone bill, thereby getting our phone cut off, I get surprised.

All the above happened today. I headed with a vengeance right for the main office of TelCel, our cell phone provider, the company in whose control resides all credit card sales for our stores. I finally reached the head of the line, gripped the Formica counter with both my hands (to keep them from reaching across that counter to grab the tie of a man I was sure would turn out to be someone who could and would do nothing to solve the problem his company had created for me), and started to unload this well-rehearsed tirade about his company, his family and him personally, when the man says to me, "Sonny Boy Williamson, Sonny Terry and Browny McGee, Big Bill Broonzy, Howlin' Wolf, Muddy Waters, BB King, John Lee Hooker and, the king of them all, Robert Johnson! How can I help you?"

"Huh?" was all I could manage.

He pointed at my T-shirt, featuring the image of Leadbelly, and said "Blues in king! What can I do for you?"

In much humbler language than I had rehearsed I explained the problem.

"I'll fix it now," he said, tapping a few keys on his keyboard and saying, "There! Your phone is back on."

I thanked him warily, edged my way slowly backwards to the door, and stepped back out into the bright sun of Mexico.

One of Milan's favorite stories he didn't need to recount to tell Mocean. Mocean lived it with him. Milan wrote about a trip they took together from Cuba back to Mexico.

The 41-foot sailboat Antares lay unattended in Havana's Marina Hemingway for eight months before our arrival. Her main engine was frozen, her stays dangerously corroded, and her cupboards bare.

My son, Mocean, and I signed on with my friend, Pepe Lima, to sail Antares back to Mexico's Yucatan knowing none of the above. But, ask yourself, are minor nuisances like these worth more than a flash of concern when, after 40 years of burning desire to stomp upon the tierra of Cuba, you find yourself strolling the streets of historic Havana Vieja, or ogling the living auto museum (every 40s car your grammar school teachers ever drove to work and every hot late-50s Chevy your hormone-saturated teenage body said was the 2-door key to sexual ecstasy) or dancing yourself breathless to the rhythmic tsunami of a 10-woman band called Lady Salsa? And the muchachas, amigos, las muchachas! No puedo explicar.

The diving? The diving alone made me forget my name.

Pristine reefs, I mean like un-fucking-touched by an anchor or chain in centuries. Huge fans, 100-plus-year-old barrel sponges you and your entire family could live in, fish that accept you as their own and school with you, 100 feet visibility, underwater canyons and caves with names like The Labyrinth, Paradise Lost and Maria's Breasts.

The condition of the boat Antares was of little concern when as a closet communist for most of my adult life (after a brief fling on the freshman dance floor with the FBI) I wanted to know as much as possible about this Cuban experiment. Racial harmony and public health and education were the obvious successes: one hundred percent literacy throughout the country, talented children recognized at early age and encouraged and educated in their fields for free (especially in areas where we gringos hardly ever raise a dime, like music, poetry, art and obscure sciences). Free medical care, free medicine, too.

But the downside (obviously affected by the US embargo, Uncle Russia's cutting off the cash flow and now, worse than ever, the inhuman Helms-Burton Act which affects only the poor and not Castro or the other Party fat cats): the country's hurting bad from severe poverty. Medicine is free but there ain't none on the shelves to be had. Star musicians who tour internationally, appear regularly on TV, and have best-selling CDs, receive only one hundred dollars per month and that's way more than doctors, engineers and scientists get.

I was stunned to discover that our dive guide has the equivalent of a PhD in theoretical physics but can't find employment in his first love, so he dives daily for the odd tip he or may not receive.

After a week of this extreme-joy/deep-sadness, it was the morning of departure and time to focus on the crossing. Pepe had flown back to Mexico and brought cable to replace the stays and an outboard motor to replace the main engine (which he bolted onto a bracket he'd welded in a nearby shop) and he and Mocean replaced the rigging while I shopped for food and water. We didn't have charts yet, which bothered me because I'm a self-proclaimed control freak when it comes to sea passages, but Pepe assured me it was but a 48-hour trip, so I shopped for 96 hours of food/water instead.

Finally, late afternoon, the guy showed up with the charts and we motored over to the Harbor Master for a final inspection by Customs, Immigration and the bad boys, Coast Guard (whose job is to prevent Cubans from escaping).

Under sail we slipped through the buoys out into the open Atlantic under a cloud-fringed sky that was rapidly tightening on us like a noose around a condemned man's neck. Two hours out of Havana harbor this storm hammered us, soaking us all so thoroughly I put on my wetsuit and dive mask just to steer. We reefed the main, flew the storm jib and did our best to buy sea room from the coast. Fortunately it was only a two-hour thick line squall and the night soon settled into a smooth sail.

Next morning an odd thing occurred: an owl (known in many cultures, like Mexican, as an omen of impending doom) circled us, landed on the back stay and stared down on us ominously for what seemed hours. During the owl's vigil I dashed below to study these charts I'd not yet seen and, lo and behold, I was looking at not a 48-hour journey but a full – if everything went perfect – five-day crossing from Cuba to the Yucatan. Most troublesome on the charts was a hardly noticeable nasty little arrow indicating a 3.5 knot current moving from the southeast (the Caribbean under Cuba) to the northwest (the center of the Gulf of Mexico).

Clearly, if anything went wrong with the wind (which Pepe assured me was a trade that blows steady from the SE) we would drift way north of the Yucatan into the Gulf.

Survival synapses began to sparkle in my head, so I called a meeting with Mocean and Pepe to discuss the obvious: we had to ration food and water because even though I'd bought double what I thought were our needs, we were already under-rationed. We talked too about the boat's batteries, how without an engine to recharge them it was only a matter of time before they went dead and that meant losing the GPS and the radio for, God forbid, the mayday we might have to send should we need to throw in the towel. Even though we're in heavily trafficked freighter lanes, we can't use our running lights at night for fear of draining the batteries.

Once we cleared the western tip of Cuba, Murphy took full command of the passage: the wind died altogether, the auxiliary outboard crapped out, and the 3.5-knot current swung in upon us. We did everything from re-rigging the sails to all configurations we could think of, to wetting the sails, to whistling to the winds.

Nothing.

Not a puff.

It's like equatorial doldrums out there.

We drifted north, farther and farther away from either land.

We're down to tiny sips of water instead of the gulps we really want and we're splitting cups of Ramen noodles instead of swallowing them whole as our bodies demand. Finally, on the fifth morning out, we vote to hide our pride as sailors and with our last drop of juice in the batteries call out a mayday to a freighter whose tower we barely see over the horizon. A Russian responds and agrees to radiophone Pepe's father in Isla Mujeres (near Cancun) with our position and condition in hopes that he'll send some sort of help.

A couple hours later, with the very last drop of battery power we hail another distant freighter and he confirms that Pepe's father did receive the call and is working on sending help. We are now over one hundred miles north of the Mexican coast, out of Mexico's territorial water, and chances are slim that anybody's navy is coming after us, so we hope Pepe's father has found a large enough fishing boat to fetch us.

And we wait. And wait. And wait for the whole day not knowing.

And while I'm lying in the cockpit in the shade of the canopy, a swallow, a beautifully colored little critter – yellow breasted, red throated, turquoise backed swallow – flies in out of nowhere (what's a swallow doing in the middle of the ocean?) and lands on my cheek. I'm not much into Cosmic Woo-Woo, but the little guy seemed a fitting symmetry to the owl on the Cuban side. He perched upon my cheekbone for twenty minutes, his little feet so cool on my skin, his soft chirp so pleasant in my ear; it seemed to me he was whispering a clear message: "Not to fret."

Sure enough, just before we suck the last drop of water from the last bottle, here comes the Mexican Navy over the horizon. They steam alongside, launch a Zodiac with six swabbies and some gifties from the cook.

(Pepe, a Mexican who has been out of Mexico for four months buries his face in the tortillas and nearly weeps).

We know now that Pepe's father called his father who called one of his best friends who happens to be the Admiral of the Mexican Navy, and that's how we were reached so (relatively) quickly. After a 22-hour tow we were back in Isla Mujeres at Pepe's grandfather's table enjoying a gourmet meal and attempting to consume all the cerveza on the island.

I'm gonna cool it on the adventure front for a while. If you need me, look for me around one of the taco stands here in Vallarta.

Life for Milan in Puerto Vallarta, where he founded a successful business that outlived him, and the mountain village where he found his dream ranch, was its own adventure, as this dispatch from El Tuito makes clear.

El Tuito is in the midst of the twelve days of celebration/pilgrimages for La Virgen de Guadalupe. The whole town and all the villages near it have drunk deep from the vat of history and come up... well... very pious, but even drunker and extremely noisy.

Yoli tells me that these "special" twelve days of La Virgen in January (when all the rest of Mexico celebrates them in December) began here in El Tuito when they completed the road from Tomatlan, to the south of El Tuito, to Vallarta in the north. The church here in Tuito discovered that all the locals suddenly began boarding buses to attend the grander ceremonies in either Tomatlan or Vallarta and that left Tuito's church with piss-poor offerings in the plato. In a stroke of genius that must have felt like a thunderbolt of divine revelation, the Bishopric decided to let the most devout make their pilgrimages to either Tomatlan or Vallarta in December and then to host the same celebration all over again here in Tuito in January.

It was a stroke of marketing genius that rivals Aspirin's "Just take two" logo. No one is asking, "Hey, how come one won't do?" And, like Aspirin doubled its sales overnight, the Bishopric scores twice.

The day beings at 4:30 am with the timid ting-ting-da-ding of a good sized bell and immediately escalates through the dong-dong-da-dong of a larger thicker bell to the womp-womp-da-womp of way more metal than should be hanging above people's heads and when that's done someone lights a string of firecrackers that would make Peking jealous and launches them from the church roof (which is only a few meters away as the cucaracha crawls from my bedroom) in an aerial display of rockets that makes Fort Sumter and the trenches of Dunkirk seem silent.

Howard Hesseman, Wavy Gravy, Lisa Law and Sevren Darden and Milan

If that ain't enough, by 4:45 am they do it all over again on the half hour until Mass is finished at 6:30 am, which is when, of all things, all the Mariachi musicians (?) in town begin their door-to-door trombone and tuba torturing, guitar gutting, and bass drum banging to raise money to complete the second spire on the church.

I am faced with a moral dilemma: how do I get these well-meaning off-key cats off my stoop without shelling out any pesos to complete the second spire from which will be hung a bell that will make the womp-womp-de-womp sound like ting-ting-a-ling?

I fold and pay. Fifty pesos. Fifty bricks closer to heaven and about an hour of deep sleep until the parades start.

People walked all night long from remote villages to reach the church's altar and cough up cash in return for a sprinkle of water.

Off to work I go, back in the late afternoon to find the streets closed. Street vendors have set up camp and are hawking everything from fundamental supplies like pots, saddles, shoes and blankets to *calientes* – hot chocolate drinks laced with cane sugar alcohol. I buy a plastic figurine of a Catholic monk who – when you press down on his head – produces an erection from under his robe. Given the scene, it's the funniest thing I've seen.

And now to bed. It's only a few hours until the dreaded ting.

Sweet dreams,

Milano del Tuito

Milan loved to tell jokes. He sent me this one from his Mexico paradise.

Heard the one about the disheveled old emigrant from Minsk who shuffles in to a very high-class brothel in NY?

"I'd like to see Natalia," he says to the madam.

"Sorry, old man, but look at your old clothes and tattered shoes. Surely you can't afford the $1,000 a night she charges."

"I have the money," says the old man as he shows the thousand dollars to the madam.

The madam leads him to Natalia's room. The old man pays Natalia and enjoys a night of bliss with the young girl.

Next night the old man appears again at the madam's door.

"Listen, old man, we offer no discounts for repeat visits. Natalia still costs $1,000 per night."

"I have the money," says the old man as he flashes the wad and walks past the madam to Natalie's room, where he pays her and spends another blissful night.

The following night the old man appears again and simply flashes the wad at the madam and goes right to Natalia's room.

During small talk the next morning Natalia remarks on what a polite customer the old man is and how surprised she is that an apparently destitute old man can afford to pay her such money; then she asks him "Where are you from, old man?"

"Minsk," he replies

"Minsk?" she responds happily. "I'm from Minsk! I have family there. My father still lives. Benjamin Petrovski. Do you know him?"

"Very well," says the old man. "He gave me three thousand dollars to give you."

One of the new adventures Mexico offered Milan was deep sea diving. Underwater was a new world, as he made clear in these notes.

Occasionally the waters of the Pacific are clear and visibility is 50+ feet. Yesterday was one of those days. We were diving a rock, El Morro, a lone pinnacle out of this Bay of Banderas in the open ocean. We were four, three experienced born-in-the-water local dive masters – I don't go down with rookies no more – and me. They led me through a long cave at about 100-foot depth, our lamps lit walls laced with 6-7-foot long moray eels.

We popped out the other side to discover a manta ray gliding overhead, wing span somewhere in the 10-foot range. He (she?) followed us back through this underwater canyon and stayed near as we slowly ascended. Once we were up to 40-foot level a half dozen more mantas cruised in to play with us. Magnificent beasts, a couple up to 14-foot wing span, each individually marked. We divers rolled around under them, imitating their flying wings with our flapping arms. We splayed out on our backs letting our bubbles tickle their bellies. And talked to them, yelling through our regulators for them to come closer and they did. Much closer. And we petted them and cavorted like otters. I was damn near weeping with joy in my mask. One by one we exhausted our air and had to return to the surface. But there's always tomorrow and the boat leaves at 8 with my ass on it.

A day later:

Yesterday's encounter was even better. I'm convinced they come to stay and play. One in particular kept edging closer and closer, then sliding off to the side, turning in front of us slipping under us and presenting his/her back to us. She lingered so long that Genaro and I could not refuse the piggyback ride she seemed to be offering. Once over the top of her I measured her wingspan (with my arms) to be 15+ feet. Genaro took hold of a pilot fish attached to her, I took hold of Genaro's tank valve and our slow-motion dance with the "devil fish" began. Must have lasted 10 minutes. We toured much of the reef under her power, then she slowly started to descend, gliding in a wide gentle spiral down from about 30 to 103 ft., which is where we hopped off.

Something tells me this stresses the beast but I'm not sure. Her behavior in the beginning led me to feel she was enjoying the play and then, when she got bored with us, she signaled us by descending to where she knew we'd let go. Thus, my need to know more.

So Milan found an expert academic and began a typical correspondence. He asked for literature, the scientist posed questions back to Milan.

Any information about the animals in your area would be very important to my work. Do you see animals of two different color patterns? CHEVRON mantas are black on top with white shoulder patches and often a white "V" extending from the "wings" and pointing toward the tail. BLACK mantas are all black on top. What is the ratio of the two color types? Males vs. females? Are there any little guys (less than 5 feet from wing tip to wing tip)? Do you have any photos of animals? Photos of the bellies of the animals would be very useful.

And Milan responded.

To be honest, I haven't put all the images together yet. I don't know what to look for yet. That's one of the reasons I want info. But I can guarantee there are tons of little guys, sometimes as small as 18 in. across. They tend to fly up out of the water, singly or two or three at a time, and flap their wings midair, then slap back down into the water.

We've seen other juveniles, probably four feet to seven feet across do these flips up into the air and fall on their backs into the water, too.

Occasionally we'll see what we think are full adults cruising just below the surface, sometimes with one wing tip above the surface. It is very common for boats to hit them, inflicting damage, I'm sure, with their outboards. Some boat captains don't even lock down their engines for fear of ripping out their transoms.

As far as which is a Chevron or a Black or a male or female, I can't yet tell the difference. They all seem to be individually marked on the belly side at least. They're so distinct that I'm sure I could begin to recognize individuals after another sighting or two. Most appear to be dark brown and the few times I've been directly over the top of them (I once rode one by grabbing onto a sucker fish attached to its back – maybe this is a no-no, I dunno, it's another reason I crave info), their hide appeared to be dark brown. The texture of their skin looked like tiny pine needles, almost like a well-coiffed, fine-quilled porcupine.

But what got me was how they seemed to want to interact with us. Obviously they could have split at any time but they circled us continually and took turns coming in close to us and stalling, almost like we were supposed to do something like clean them or have sex or I dunno what. But we could call them and they would respond and come in closer.

It's really something!

I'm told by local guys in my dive group that they are here during the same time the whales are (and the Bay of Banderas is packed with them now, too).

Sorry, don't have any photos or gear to get them with. Why don't you fly down? It's only around $400 from SFO. Spend a long weekend or something. We could put you up in the spare bedroom and I can arrange free dive trips out there.

Meantime, do get me whatever info you can at whatever cost and tell me what you look for and I'll pump info your way.

Best,

Milan

In Mexico, Milan continued to plot and scheme. While working for a Cancun diving company, he came up with this plan.

I propose we purchase a military aircraft, specifically a Russian MIG, and sink it as an artificial reef in a place and at a depth that would serve as both a "Wreck Dive" and a "Deep Dive" for us. Prior to sinking the aircraft, large indestructible letters should be welded onto the fuselage which read: "For your diving pleasure! Courtesy of AquaWorld!"

Therefore, any other dive company that took clients to the wreck would be promoting AquaWorld.

Costs for the purchase, transport, and sinking of the MIG could be covered by an inexpensive publicity campaign involving small advertisements in all the major dive magazines in North America, Europe and Asia, which read simply: "Help us sink a Russian MIG. Contact www.aquaworld.com.mx"

We can expect a tremendous amount of inquiries.

Milan's idea was to charge 50 people a thousand dollars for the adventure.

Currently we have two options to purchase a MIG. Joe Vittone has located two MIGs in the Ukraine and negotiated a price of $5,000 per aircraft. I met and gave a tour of our facilities to an official of the Cuba Ministry of Tourism, who also said she could arrange the purchase of a Russian MG from the Cuban government.

Since Cuba is so much closer, I propose I fly there as soon as possible, begin the negotiating for the purchase of a MIG, and investigate transportation costs.

To be the first company on the planet to sink a Russian MIG for the purposes of recreational diving would generate worldwide publicity and create a flood of editorial articles that could not be purchased.

Let's do it!

Milan moved his headquarters up to Puerto Vallarta and founded the thriving business he left when he died: importing sarongs from Bali to sell to the endless planeloads of North Americans and Europeans arriving daily at Mexican resorts. During his last weeks Milan worked hard to insure that the business would continue without him, as this email makes clear.

Date: Tue, 28 Aug 2001
From: Milan in Mexico
Subject: UPDATE

Today marks the 21st day since I got The Word and much has transpired.

First of all, I've opted not to go with the chemo. The more I found out about it, the less I liked the idea. You know the deal: for openers, it's effective in only 30 percent of cases, its side-effects are totally debilitating and often injurious to the existing immune system and, worst of all, it impacts one's quality of life to such a negative degree that I decided not to draw from the deck but to stick with the cards I've been dealt. Given the Hepatitis C lurking behind all this other stuff, I don't want to hammer my body with chemicals that might remove what resistance I retain. The fact is, nobody's ever been "cured" of Stage 4 pancreatic cancer on the level that I have it, so I'd rather enjoy two months of relative bliss than drag my sorry ass thru two years of hell. Quality, not quantity, is what we're after here.

The good news is that I've probably got way more than two months anyway and with the naturopathy program I'm on – diet and dietary supplements designed to lessen growth of cancer cells while increasing growth of NK (natural killer) cells, which nibble away at the cancer, I stand a far better chance of enjoying the time I have left. And this diet works! I've stopped the weight loss, have a healthy appetite, lots of energy and very positive mood. That's all I should ask for at this stage, no?

Come to think of it, good news abounds. After dealing with my own demons about death and dying, my biggest worry was for the mini-world I would leave behind, specifically, the Pareos business, Georgeanne and Yoli and Mocean.

And it couldn't be better on the business front. Janelle has been here for 5 days now and we've had daily meetings that have run the gamut from heart-wrenching, tear-jerking soul-searching to nitpicky Virgo business details. It's very clear to me that this big bucks distribution system I've created here in Mexico is very healthy and will (in combination with Georgeanne's production system in Bali) continue to provide a healthy livelihood for hundreds of people far into the future.

Georgeanne has fully accepted Yoli and Janelle, my sister, as business partners and she's accepted Yoli as the woman in whose arms I will eventually cack and, probably needless to say, both decisions make my heart soar.

Yesterday we all ended up on Rancho Santa Rosa in El Tuito – Yoli, her two kids, Yoli's mother and sister, Georgeanne, Janelle, and me. As the morning drew on I was able to physically withdraw to an isolated rooftop and watch these people grow together and relate to one another without me as the catalyst. Yoli and Georgeanne strolling the rose gardens together, sharing tips and clippings and spontaneously embracing was the high point and literally took my breath away. I realized at this moment that I can pass on as happy, proud, and guilt-free as anyone can expect to be.

Now that the biz meetings are almost over, Georgeanne and Janelle will return to the States and I will be able to settle into a groove of writing my way out of this and, simultaneously, dreaming of The Last Dive: the Galapagos islands off Ecuador, the Cocos off Costa Rica jump to mind immediately, but Maria La Gorda in Cuba might warrant another visit, too. We'll see.

I'll be in closer touch from here on out.

Love to you all,

Milan

14

ADIOS

And it was from Mexico that he sent his last message, October 6, 2001.

Dear Family and Friends,

Please be informed that I have crossed over to the other side or as some say "gone paws up" or "assumed room temperature." It was a Hellaciously painful six-month ordeal for me, made tolerable by your kind words and warm wishes.

Not knowing, of course, what's on the other side, I promise you that if there is anything ever in eternity that I can do for you from there, I'll get it done. But if the Tibetan Buddhists have it right, I'll be back around after forty-nine days for another go at learning the lessons I flunked this time. Look for the little boy in the Cowboy and Indian pajamas with the pith helmet and safari jacket and know that Expedition Melvin rides again!

In closing, let me ask that you think of me as having a First Class seat on the nonstop Bullet Train to the greatest Mystery and the grandest Adventure of all.

YEE-HA!

YEE-HA!

And love,

Milan.

AFTERWORDS

Among the friends getting that message were Howard Hesseman, Alan Myerson and Carl Gottlieb, who responded with their memories when I passed along Milan's request that they write of their times with Milan for this volume. Mike Wilhelm, a founding member of The Charlatans, volunteered memories for this second edition. I found it impossible to find anyone who encountered Milan who does not have a story to tell, and usually those stories start with lines like, "Before I met Milan I'd never.. . ." or "The first time I ever (fill in the blank) was with Milan . . ." or "Milan convinced me to (fill in the blank), it changed my life. . ." Hesseman, Myerson, and Gottlieb had more than their share of Milan stories to tell.

Hesseman filed this from Paris.

Foreword! – or more precisely, ¡Forward! – seems a proper kick-start for any discussion of Milan Melvin's life. Here was a man who seemed only at ease wherever he might be. The itch to move on to the next place, the next adventure was an animating inner force equal to his interest in – and engagement with – present surroundings. While deeply involved in the moment, his head and heart were simultaneously perhaps halfway around the world as he envisioned future itineraries and activities.

Five marriages in a 58-year life span bespeak an urge to move on to new things, do they not? In addition to an inventive way with English, a fluency in Spanish, French, a fair command of Thai, Nepalese, and Tibetan, plus a more than passing acquaintance with Balinese and Russian would indicate a desire to learn, to exchange information and ideas. Milan's dogged pursuit of new experiences was stunning in its consistency. He could barely conceal his delight in circumventing the official way of doing things by testing the authority of conventional wisdom. Although christened Milan Morrell Melvin, actions and attitude often suggested the hero who mentions, in an intensely casual manner, "Danger is my middle name."

This guy needed a much longer run, yet never backed off reducing his chances if it meant passing on a rush.

We met in 1966 in the socio-pharmaceutical ferment that was San Francisco. He had recently moved there from Virginia City, Nevada, then a small but smoldering hotbed of gun-toting Old West hippie fantasists who took Hank Williams at his word and tried "Settin' the Town on Fire."

With a wide variety of chemical stimulation, they nightly burned down their brains, if not the town, by turning the historic Gold Rush-era Red Dog Saloon into a rock 'n' roll dance hall.

Milan decided to mosey on down the trail after a spell, and eventually took up the slack in an apartment I'd sublet to two fellow actors in The Committee, San Francisco's famed improvisational-political cabaret theater company, replacing one who was headed back to NYC. The apartment was the top floor of a wood-framed house with a mean lean, built in the 1880s atop hand-cut logs still visible as its foundation, by my aging landlord's grandfather, a mason who'd laid brick in the original portion of the Ghirardelli Chocolate Factory just across the street.

1967 saw the birth of underground FM rock 'n' roll radio, as Tom "Big Daddy" Donahue and a group of slightly warped DJs, both professional and amateur, infiltrated a local multicultural-formatted FM station, introducing a new approach to radio, first slipping into expired time slots between, say, the Top 10 Polka Review and the Latvian Antler-dance Show. As one of three members of The Committee moonlighting (for ten bucks a shift) as weekend on-air anti-personalities, my Saturday afternoon shift followed several hours of classic Chinese opera. We were all far more focused on the music than the sound of our own voices – or so it seemed.

Milan met Tom D, and immediately became the station's advertising sales manager. A rapid boost in finances followed, as Milan correctly reasoned that the hot accounts for this newly created and peculiar listener base would be outside the mainstream. Suddenly, numerous waterbed stores, head shops, exotic eateries, recycled clothing/furniture/knick-knack emporiums, health food stores, and the odd Volvo dealership were experiencing a noticeable increase in customers, reflecting reciprocity from their investment in this self-styled outlaw operation. Milan was also involved in producing a number of local dance concerts as part of a consortium of whacked wanna-dance wizards under the subtly subversive handle, "The Western Front."

Within a year, he had moved on another front, too; he entered into his third marriage, keeping it within the extended family so counterculturally *au courant* at the time; his bride was a member of The Committee. At this point, he sublet from me a second time, as I was performing in a Committee company on the Sunset Strip in LA. The post-honeymoon cottage he scored? Pre-earthquake, redwood-shingled, fireplace, deck w/view of Bay Bridge, Treasure and Yerba Buena Islands, set on the unique, gardened steps of Telegraph Hill's eastern slope – a fairly fantasy-fulfilling little crib in the rich mix of SF habitation. But relative domesticity was to last little over a year before he announced to me that he was "splitting the sheets."

He promptly divorced his third wife, and shortly thereafter crossed the US on his beloved Harley as Wagon Master, riding at the head of a caravan of buses highly decorated in psychedelic style. The lead bus carried Tom Donahue – along with Milan, a prime instigator of this cross-country prank – and announced across its broad expanse of grill, "We have come for your daughters!" This very odd odyssey lasted a month or so, during which frequent stops involved the presentation of R 'n' R concerts staged adjacent to major cities where the caravan had pitched its teepees – the entire venture being filmed as a feature-length musical documentary to be released by Warner Bros. (As mentioned, Big Daddy was rarely far from this kind of action. And from WB's POV, how could it miss? Hippies! Hippie buses! Hippie teepees! Sex, Drugs & Rock 'n' Roll, together at last and On The Road, as well as at a theater near you! To this day, you have to see it – *Medicine Ball Caravan* – to disbelieve it.)

With a number of caravaners in tow (on WB's dime), Milan continued on to England for presentation of the final concert. With the thoroughly twisted tour concluded and his Harley running well, it seemed only natural to squirrel around Europe and North Africa for a few months. While living in Asila, then but a tiny fishing village on Morocco's Atlantic coast, his ever-alert ear caught a mega-memorable multilingual utterance from a fisherman friend, gazing out at the sea: "By Allah! Le Mer is no fuckin' bueno today!"

Milan returned briefly to California, only to quickly set an easterly course, announcing his determination to explore Asia before McDonalds, Baskin & Robbins, etc., established any beachheads. He started in Kathmandu (and started all over again with another marriage), setting up a day-care center for children of Tibetan refugees, freeing their parents to weave traditional rugs, which he then transported, along with many tasty Tibetan artefacts, to the US on frequent visits. Using his own funds, he published the first comprehensive, conversationally-oriented English-Tibetan dictionary. A few years of trekking and trading in the no-man's land twixt Nepal and China's Tibetan "zone," and lowland life began to exert a pull. Suddenly, it seemed he was refitting a traditional Chinese junk, avowing to sail the China Seas.

Random movements dictated by wind, tides, and reports of real, armed pirates in the vicinity ensued for a while. Then, anchored offshore from Bangkok, he and his wife delivered his son Mocean unassisted.

Friends shortly thereafter received a blow-by-blow birth announcement, for Milan had made a running audio commentary of the event with a cassette recorder and sent copies to all. Feeling the need for more stability beneath his family's feet, Milan et al settled in Bali.

Throughout this Asian foray, he also managed to visit large portions of India. His wife experienced a spiritual awakening and decided to stay in India. Divorced and returning Stateside, he ended up refurbishing one of the oldest houseboats moored at Sausalito's Gate 5, where he resided for less than a year before The Traveler's Itch got to him again. Then, for the third time, I passed a place on to him, this time – having "inherited" it from another Committee actor – a classic Hollywood bungalow.

Okay – time for a little breather! At least you now have a quick culling of high points from the first 15 years of our friendship. It continued for another 20 years. How much space am I allotted here, in which to merely suggest what my old amigo was up to during that time? Not that he was always alone; am I to skip the tales of our laugh-packed yet all too intermittent travels together in the USA, and to Paris, Mexico, Italy, South Africa, Russia? And more to the point – how to describe his joy in experiencing all these adventuresome fantasies coming to pass? How to make you taste his experience, feel the racing pulse of his excitement, share the insightful and fun-filled point of view he offered in personal terms about all this?

He never relented from his belief that you had to follow your dreams, and that the first thing to do about that was to just do something to get underway. There was much history to be researched and respected, but there were few paths to be rigorously followed, as he was convinced by experience that you served yourself and perhaps others by carving out new ones. He was, thankfully, a faithful correspondent.

Many of us came to think of him as "Expedition" Melvin, ecstatic each time in the exotic luxury of a new culture/landscape/friend, eagerly sharing his experiences on paper with pals far more comfortable in less far-flung circumstances. See, I'm fortunate, for I still have some of his letters – like the one reporting his Moroccan fisherman's remarkably mangled weather report. Perhaps I've been daydreaming, but I just remembered that Milan, in the last week of his all-too-short life, entrusted his journals to Peter Laufer, and it would seem you're holding the result in your hands. So, when it comes to learning something about Milan's deeds and thoughts as he did what he did, I guess you're about to discover something for yourself. He would have wanted it that way.

Howard Hesseman, 2001

This from Alan Myerson:

Milan Melvin. What to say about him? He said much of it himself and others have said most of the rest. Clearly rare, the man stood tall and loved it – in fact, I think part of his journey and race was to try to find ways to get taller. Or, at least, higher.

I knew him for more than thirty-five years – through gunplay, Harleys, machismo (which goes without saying) and all that implies, courtliness, travel, contraband, rock & roll, entrepreneurship, a few marriages and other entanglements, fuck-ups and grace, guidance and confusion, story-telling, a lot of hustles, ambition and, of course, of course, ADVENTURES! Does anyone think it coincidental or unconscious that in his last written words to the world he capitalized "Mystery" and "Adventure"?

In spite of his ebullience and swagger Milan also possessed a mighty reticence, which is a quality I share. I think that similarity may have been one of the strands in whatever particular connection we felt with each other. I traveled to exotic places with him, took drugs with him, argued, joked, wrote with him, schemed, cursed and celebrated whatever we thought was going on at the time, pushed and pulled with him. If you knew Milan well, probably you could and would say the same. Certainly, he was generous in spreading himself around. And those of us who knew him well all have some story or experience that was unique – that was part of what you got with Milan.

Anyway, here's mine:

One night in the late '60s I got a call in LA from Milan who was in San Francisco. (I was splitting my time between the two cities with Committee companies in both places.) He needed to see me and it was very important!

"Cool," I said, "I'll be up there on Tuesday."

"No, man, that's too late! I need to see you sooner."

"Well, Milan, I can't get up there before then."

"Okay," he said, "Can I come down tomorrow morning and see you there?"

So, he did – travel never daunted him. Around ten the next morning a cab pulled up to the house and Milan and Mimi Farina got out. We sat down and either drank or smoked some tea and Milan announced that he and Mimi were getting married. Now, I was married but for the moment I was envious – he had a way of inducing envy in many of us. But, I congratulated them and said that, flashy as the news was, I thought it could have waited till Tuesday. However, it turned out his wedding announcement was not the purpose of this call.

This was: it seems that the night before, in order to create an honest basis for their marriage, Mimi suggested they reveal to each other whatever secrets they thought they might have been keeping. And, in an unaccustomed burst of candor, when Milan told Mimi one of his secrets she insisted he needed to tell me immediately. So, now they were sitting in my kitchen as he told me that, when he was an undergraduate at Berkeley, he had signed up to be an FBI informant spying on left-wing student politics (I don't recall where in his resume this occurred – pre- or post-Hell's Angels – but it definitely predated acid, Peace/Love/We've Come For Your Daughters, and really long hair). The notion of Milan being a snitch was so outlandish it was hard to believe, but then he got even more uptight. It seems the really sticky part of all this was that he had been specifically assigned to keep tabs on a particular leader of Berkeley's many civil rights and anti-HUAC demonstrations. He didn't know how to say it – but his target had been my brother.

What's a hippie to do? Mimi was looking sad and hopeful, Milan was looking contrite, so I looked forgiving. In fact, he seemed so contrite I gave him a beautiful, treasured and very valuable old woven southwestern Indian basket/stash-box which he received gratefully. I think. I was never sure if the gratitude was for the box or the forgiveness – or if the contrition was just instantaneous Milan-in-the-Moment. He was a complicated dude.

That was a long time ago and many other things passed between us as we passed and caught up with each other over and over again. I was privileged to be with him for part of the last week he spent in this particular life and I'm glad of virtually all the times I ever spent with him. They were sometimes mixed blessings, sometimes pure – just like Milan.

Alan Myerson, 2001

And this from Carl Gottlieb:

Here's a long, rambling narrative, a story I've told often, usually while trying to explain the Sixties to people who weren't born (or conscious) then. It's about how Milan and I first became friends, and it's an exercise in nostalgic recollection. Thanks in advance for indulging my memories. (Howard, if I'm wrong, back me up on this).

In Autumn of 1966, Milan and I had been introduced once or twice at parties or after-show drinks at Enrico's, our common acquaintance being a Hollywood casting director named Fred Roos, who thought Milan was an interesting "type." Milan had aspirations to work as an actor, being dramatic looking and all, with shoulder-length hair and Fu Manchu moustache. He had gotten 8 x 10 glossy photos of himself, in hippie cowboy regalia with real guns, probably left over from the summer of 1966 at the Red Dog Saloon in Virginia City, where everyone lived in psychedelic Wild West/Mountain Man/Saloon Girl dress-up.

Fred Roos went on to become a producer of note ("Godfather II") and had a long association with Francis Coppola) but at that time he was casting director for several Paramount sit-coms and often came to San Francisco. He was the first Hollywood guy to exploit the comedy talents at the Committee – a bunch of undiscovered mad improvisers who were happy to work for scale.

Roos' intros were brief; Milan and I got on well, but without any real connection beyond "He seems like a good guy." and "Want a hit of this?"

In the winter of 1966 I went to LA to work in a failed pilot, and was eating breakfast one morning around 11 am at the original Hamburger Hamlet. It was then a small café on the Strip, a block west of the Whiskey a Go Go, with a weathered plank outdoor patio, where I was sitting alone.

Along comes Milan, walking on Sunset Boulevard. I say, "Hi." He says, "Hi." We're both San Francisco psychedelic expatriates in plastic LA. We sit down for breakfast together. During the course of the meal, I learned that Milan had to vacate his pad in the Fillmore and needed a place to crash when he went back in a few days' time. I had a few more weeks to work in LA, so I offered him my place, a pad on North Point Street, across the street from Ghirardelli Square.

Milan needed a place, I had a place, so without a second thought I wrote down the address and gave him the keys to my house – that was the Sixties for you. If a guy had really long hair and smoked dope, you could trust him with your life. Not quite as naïve as it sounds; if you had long hair in January 1967, it meant that you started not cutting it in 1965, which made it hard for undercover narcs to "blend in" with the pot-dealing underground of which Milan was a charter member (Berkeley, Castlemont High School, cousin Bobby).

The place itself was cool – a funky handmade North Beach wood-frame clapboard house built before the 1906 earthquake – two cheap rental flats on top of each other in the interior courtyard of a Victorian storefront facing Ghirardelli Square, which at that time was still half occupied by a working chocolate factory, and only half-developed into the extravagant space it is now. There were a lot fewer tourists in those days.

The elderly landlord was the son of the builder, the place had been family owned by North Beach Italians since the turn of the last century, and it was $85 a month. We paid the rent to old man Giuliani, who worked in a flower shop on Columbus Avenue, near Union Street. He hung out next door to the shop at a newsstand-espresso bar with other old Italian men in hats and suspenders and shirts without collars, who smoked little stinky black cigars and worshipped photos of Joe Dimaggio, a son of local paisanos. In those days, North Beach and Upper Grant Ave. were solidly Italian from Broadway to the Embarcadero and Fisherman's Wharf. Chinatown stopped where Grant Ave. and Stockton and Kearny ran into Broadway.

I inherited the place from Larry Hankin, who got it from Howard and Kathy Hesseman. The interior partitions had been torn out, transforming a few small dark bedrooms into a large L-shaped loft-like space with one bedroom, a makeshift kitchen at one end, and a bathroom in the back, where an exterior wood staircase descended. It was a bare, spare place; I had disposed of most of the furniture before I left. This was the inventory I left behind: a nice deep-red plush carpet, the mandatory mattress and box spring on the floor, a round oak claw-foot Victorian table (you could buy them at second-hand furniture shops on Hayes Street for $90 then, a few chairs included), and some used kitchenware. And all my clothing and personal effects that weren't with me in LA.

Anyway, we shook hands and went on our way, Milan with the keys to my house (and my life) in San Francisco. He called once or twice to say he had moved his stuff into the North Point pad without incident, and asked if I minded that he had brought over a few sticks of furniture and put up some shelves for books and stereo. I said that was cool.

When I was finished in LA I returned to find my bare little studio transformed; Milan's bed on a well-constructed platform that doubled as a roomy couch in the main room, facing clean new shelving against a wall, a good stereo rig, plenty of records, more comfy chairs. It was homey.

Overnight, we were roommates, and lived together for the next two years (1967 and 1968), until I went to LA with the Committee.

Those two years together encompassed the "Summer of Love," KMPX and the invention of underground FM radio, and lots of sex, drugs and rock & roll – Janis Joplin, my few groupies, his many stewardesses, the gang from the Red Dog Saloon, the gang from the Committee, their friends, and more.

There were also bricks and bricks moving through the pad on their way from LA to Oakland and New York, which meant we never wanted for good weed. A neighbor of ours, Jerry Kamstra, even wrote a book about it later, aptly titled "Weed." It was my second adolescence (the first one didn't take), and everyone was just passing through: Rob Reiner and Richard Dreyfuss, Teri Garr, David Crosby, The Charlatans, the Loving Spoonful, even Hunter Thompson researching his Hell's Angel book. He interviewed Milan, who had a connection to the East Oakland chapter of the Angels. Hunter was an interesting asshole then, as now.

Upstairs, in the floor-through, were three women we called "The Girls Next Door." They were: belly dancer Glynn Deffry and her kid, artist and amateur topless dancer Linda Gravenides (recently divorced from blues musician Nick Gravenides, and later famous as Janis's companion and wardrobe designer) and another single mom named Serena, with a kid named Joaquin.

For a long time our routine was simple: Milan and I would roll out of bed around 10 or 11 am If either or both of us had a sleepover babe, we'd make breakfast for all of us. Milan and I both cooked and washed up afterwards, women always enjoyed watching us handle kitchen chores. If it was just me and him, we'd see if the Girls Next Door were up, share a couple of joints, then all of us would make our way across the street and onto the upper deck of the Square, where a coffeehouse called Portofino overlooked the Bay. At eleven in the morning they'd be just opening, taking chairs off the tables, firing up the espresso machine, and we'd snag a table on the rail, with Ghirardelli Square and Aquatic Park spread out before us.

There we'd share the *Chronicle*, read Herb Caen's column and the funnies, order fresh hot chocolate, cappuccinos, and croissants, and watch ships and seagulls through tinted glasses while our high spiraled gently down. That's how our days started, and most of the time they got better as they went on.

Six nights a week the day's climax was the nightly performance at The Committee, where I acted with a troupe of improvisers who were a family. We were a talented, contentious, fractious, loving, creative family that differed in only one way from a clan related by blood: we took turns being the idiot half-wit cousin – it wasn't a role in which we were trapped by an accident of birth.

My Committee friends then are my extended family today. They are the people with whom I share Thanksgiving dinners, regular dinners, some holidays, and with depressingly increasing frequency, funerals and memorial services. Milan was with us then, and his memory stays with us now. Speaking for myself, that'll be true as long as "now" keeps becoming "then."

Carl Gottlieb, 2001

Mike Wilhelm, lead guitarist with The Charlatans, the first of the Sixties psychedelic San Francisco bands, remembers:

I first met Milan in Berkeley during 1963 when I arrived in the Bay Area from Los Angeles. I had been playing surf guitar in Danny Clapp and the Bangers, the house band at the Monkey Inn, a UC frat boy hang-out. After our gig we'd usually go get hamburgers at Tingo's on University, which was open all night. Milan was the night staff, taking orders and grilling burgers.

The Charlatans were playing at the Red Dog Saloon when Milan arrived during the summer of '65. His hair was considerably longer but his face was unmistakable. I told him I remembered him from Tingo's a couple of years before. He said he remembered our crew coming there three or four nights a week.

His girlfriend Zella was a cocktail waitress at the Red Dog. Richard Olsen had been Zella's place-holder until Milan arrived and was kind of upset when Milan arrived to claim her... took him a bit to recover from that one. Milan was a perfect fit at the Red Dog. He was making leather goods and such. He rode a Harley XLCH Sportster, as I recall.

Mike Wilhelm, 2015

When Joan Baez heard a new edition of Milan's autobiography was being prepared, she sent this:

At Milan's marriage to my sister Mimi in 1968, everything shone. The grass, the pines, Mimi's eyes and the ripples of sun on Milan's shoulder-length black hair as it floated around in the wind. The wreath of flowers on Mimi's head bounced lightly in time to the beating of her heart.

From that celebration came the title and inspiration for "Sweet Sir Galahad," the first song I ever wrote.

> *Sweet Sir Galahad came down*
> *With his gay bride of flowers*
> *The prince of the hours*
> *Of her lifetime...*

Milan was kind to Mimi, at a time in her life when she needed extra love and caring. He was truly a soothing balm. Lean, lanky, self-contained, charming, and a natural gentleman – one of a dying breed even then.

Sometimes, I sit quietly sipping some tea and talk to him, as I do periodically with people I love who have crossed over. He always liked a good cup of tea.

> *And here's to the dawn of their days...*
> *Of their days.*

Joan Baez, 2015

Editor's Note (to first edition):
The publication date for Highlights of a Lowlife was approaching fast when, without warning, the company contracted to publish the book went bankrupt. At the time, I was working on a project in Egypt. Hoping that we could still make the Spring 2004 schedule for the book, I found a printing plant in Cairo that could take over production of the book and meet our timetable. The Internet made transfer of the editorial content immediate and flawless. However, with the bankrupt publisher consumed by his own immediate problems, the irreplaceable photographs and other memorabilia that adorn this book were misplaced. Worried that these graphic treasures would be locked up by the bankruptcy court pending resolution of the publisher's financial crisis – or worse, would be lost forever – we scrambled to secure them. After a few tense days, my wife Sheila convinced an office manager to search for the package filled with these images. They finally were located and Sheila drove to Berkeley to collect them.

A mostly full moon was rising over the Egyptian desert when my mobile rang. I was reading Miramar in a window seat of a grubby and threadbare second-class carriage on train 926 out of Masr railroad station in Alexandria, wishing the tea vendor offered California Chardonnay. It was a delighted Sheila on the line, announcing that she had secured the material: the photographs of Milan in his cowboy outfit and on his Harley, the trekking permits and passports, the hand-drawn map to the opium den.

Wherever he is, I know it makes Milan smile that the first edition of his autobiography was scheduled to be printed in Egypt (although we ultimately found a better deal in Michigan!) and that a crisis of its publication was resolved with an telephone call from Sheila in California to me on a Third World train ride from Alexandria to Cairo.

Peter Laufer, 2003

www.ingramcontent.com/pod-product-compliance
Lightning Source LLC
Chambersburg PA
CBHW070329090426
42733CB00012B/2417

The Color
of Light